As you
the miracles God has
brought into my life,
I pray that faith will
arise within your spirit
and your miracle
will come whatever
the need is.

Love In Christ,

Rose Franco

John 15:7
Matt 18:19 & 20
Prov. 11:30

A Lifetime of

Miracles

How the miracles of God can transform

Body, Mind, and Spirit!

———————

Rose Franco

Praise for
A Lifetime of Miracles

"This book is amazing! I love how Rose Franco has divided it up into miracles relating to mind, spirit and body as well as miracles of provision, revelation, by dreams and visions. As I began reading the chapter 2 about "A Doctor's Miracle" it seemed familiar. As I continued, I recalled that doctor being in our service and the blessings that resulted. I rejoiced reading the rest of the story. I am excited about her book because it is a faith builder and I will encourage all the members of our church to purchase a copy and read it. God certainly wants to perform many miracles and is looking for willing vessels like Rose. She illustrates how God can use the ordinary events of our life to do the extraordinary if we are sensitive and available. I pray this book will be an inspiration to many people.

I have known the Francos for many years since they have ministered at our church with signs and wonders following. They are the most wonderful couple and God has used them in remarkable ways. I strongly endorse their ministry, as they were regular guests at our church."

Pastor Bruce O. Klepp
Upper Room Assembly of God, Miami, FL

"Rose Franco, along with her husband John, an evangelist, has been a blessing to our church for many years. Rose has sensitivity to the Holy Spirit that allows her to prophetically impact people's lives. Her compassion and anointing while praying with people has brought healing physically and emotionally. Her book will undoubtedly inspire faith."

Pastor & Mrs. David K. Fox
Lighthouse Tabernacle Church of God, Central Islip, NY

Praise for
A Lifetime of Miracles

"What excitement and enjoyment awaits you as you peruse the pages of this book. After a lifetime of supernatural experiences, Rose Franco has compiled a book so that people everywhere may come to faith in Jesus as their Savior, Healer, Protector and Provider. Many people today seem to believe that miracles were only experienced in Bible times while others doubt the possibility that any divine intervention can be experienced by humanity. But Rose has shared from her own life many evidences of God's power to prove that miracles are happening today.

As a certified minister, pastor's wife and an active worker in the church, business and professional world, Rose experienced these miracles. Everyone who reads this book, comes to believe that God is no respecter of persons and relies on the promises of God's Word and the power of the Holy Spirit, will experience their own miracles."

John D. Johnson, Senior Pastor
Assembly of God Church, Bayshore, NY

"This is not a theoretical book. It gives actual experiences of trusting God. If you want to experience God's power, trust Him, and what you read in this book you will find occurring in your life."

Dr. N.J. Tavani, B.D., Ph. D.
Sociology Professor Emeritus, Altadena, CA

"Rose Franco has not only believed but demonstrated God's power for healing. I'm so grateful for growing up spiritually under such a faithful defender of the supernatural power of God. Her faith and her life impacted me early in my ministry. Her book will inspire you to believe for miracles today."

Dr. Ron Burgio, President - Elim Fellowship
Senior Pastor - Love Joy Gospel Church, Clarence, NY

About the Author

The author, Rose Franco holds credentials with the Assemblies of God as a licensed Certified Minister of the Gospel. She travels and ministers with her Evangelist husband John.

As a pastor's wife her life was never dull, always finding herself busy, either with her family, her job or with the church. She was director of the youth rap session in her church and Sunday school teacher for the College and Career class. She started the Bible Club at a high school in the Buffalo school district where she taught art classes including creative crafts, drawing, painting and photography.

While with the Christian Churches of North America she was director of the women's ministries, called Dorcas Fellowship of the Niagara-Mohawk District in New York State. During that time, several new fellowships as well as a newspaper entitled, "Women on the Move for Christ" were started. While co-director of the National Dorcasettes Ministry she compiled a manual for the program.

She has been the main speaker at women's retreats, special events including Women's Aglow and has been president of several women's ministry groups. She was director of several outreach ministries involved with orphanages, unwed mothers and prisons while ministering in Youngstown, Ohio.

While teaching, counseling, serving as a camp counselor, presiding president of women's ministries, taking religious studies and directing several church plays, she found time to go to college. During this time she managed to obtain a Bachelor of Science and Master of Science degrees in art education, K to college level, and certification in elementary K-6. She has an associate degree in business and has had real estate licenses in New York and Florida.

She was a member of the NYATA, an associate member of the NYSEA, and was on the scholarship awards committee at the State College of Buffalo, New York. While teaching in a college in Glendale, Arizona, she was a member of the Arizona Artist Guild and Arizona Watercolor Association.

In spite of her very active life, the role of wife, mother and grandmother has always been her first priority. The best gift that she gives to her family is her time to listen, love, share and teach the truth of God's Word without compromise. If a need arises, she is ready to give a helping hand. She has often said, "If we give our all in serving God and our family should be lost, what have we gained as godly parents?" Her greatest joy is in knowing that many of her children and grandchildren are involved in ministry.

Her ultimate desire is to be a vessel lead by the Holy Spirit to reach the lost with the message of salvation, bring the healing Word of God to the hurting and to be a blessing to those she meets along life's journey.

DEDICATION

To the living blessings from God in my life:

my children,

my grandchildren,

and my great-grandchildren.

The best words I could leave with you
are the words my mother left with me,
"Keep the Joy of the Lord in your heart
for it is your strength."

TABLE OF CONTENTS

Foreword

"In this book Rose will stir your faith and encourage you as she shares a collection of testimonies of the miracles of God, both big and small, that occur in everyday life. Rejoice with Rose in the goodness of God as you read this book. God has many miracles ready for you. Rose along with her husband has been serving in the ministry for over 50 years. Her writings come from years of wisdom gained in effective ministry from all circumstances and with all types of people. Read with openness of heart. You will hear wisdom speaking- you will be a better person for reading this book."

Pastor Phil Munsey
Life Church, Mission Viejo, CA

" 'Even when the disease became life-threatening, he did not seek the Lord's help but sought help only from his physicians. So he died.' (2 Chronicles 16:12,13 NLT) Some believe the king dies because the physicians of that day were not as advanced as our modern physicians. Today, it's easy to put faith in a doctor instead of God. God knows the root of the disease and the best way to heal it.

Rose Franco has seen first hand the power of shifting one's faith from man to God. Rose's gentle way of reminding us to give to the physician what is the physician's and to God what is God's has restored many to health. Your physician can stave off disease for a time, but the Lord is required for true long-term healing.

Rose's delivery of the good news transforms the ailing mind and heart, allowing hope and faith to enter places where only cold, hard medical jargon existed. This book is a breath of fresh air in a stagnant profession."

Dr. Jeffrey Middleton
Owner, Lord's Chiropratic and Puantum Medicine Center
Fort Lauderdale, FL

Acknowledgments

Thanks most of all, to my Lord and Savior for making this book a reality through the happenings brought about in my life by the Holy Spirit.

To my husband John, who has taken on some of my household chores to allow me freedom to spend hours writing, thanks John, for all your encouragement and for all hours spent helping to edit this book.

I want to thank my daughter, Maria Miller, who assisted me since the initial draft. This book would not have been completed without her invaluable suggestions, times of teaching me new information about the computer to ease my writing, correcting grammar, and formatting. Thanks Maria, for bringing it all together and for your patience. I pray you will reap blessings from the hearts of those who read this book.

To my son Robert, who has shared some of his writing ability with me, thanks Robert, for hours spent restructuring some of my thoughts and for designing the book cover. Thanks for the encouragement when I wanted to give up.

To my son John and his wife Jeneva, thanks for encouraging me to write the book and for saying, "Mom, you have to write your story and let people know about the miracles and answered prayers that God brought about in your life and in the lives of others!"

Thanks to my grandchildren for the part they play in my life. Their walk with the Lord inspires me as does their personal words of encouragement.

Thanks to Mrs. S. Moore, my prayer partner, for your endless prayers and encouragement, and for giving me permission to include your testimony in my book. I am also thankful for the times we prayed together and witnessed many miracles.

Many thanks go to Dr. and Mrs. Donald M. Decker from Royal Literary Publications who did a great job in helping to edit my book.

Introduction

Matthew 9:35 states, "And Jesus went about all the cities and villages, teaching in their synagogues, and preaching the gospel of the kingdom, and healing every sickness and every disease among the people." Jesus gave power to His disciples in Matthew 10:8 saying, "Heal the sick, cleanse the lepers, raise the dead, cast out devils: freely ye have received, freely give."

Miracles continued to happen in the early church after the Holy Spirit had come upon the disciples. "He that believeth on me, the works that I do shall he do also; and greater works than these shall he do; because I go unto my Father." (John 14:12). Miracles were not only for the early church but have continued throughout each following generation.

You and I are witnesses that miracles are still happening today. His Word never fails and His power never changes. "Jesus Christ the same yesterday, and today, and forever." (Hebrews 13:8).

The Word of God is the Christian's textbook. We believe what the Word of God says in James 5:14-15, "Is any sick among you? Let him call the elders of the church; and let them pray over him, anointing him with oil in the name of the Lord: And the prayer of faith shall save the sick, and the Lord shall raise him up; and if he has committed sins, they shall be forgiven him."

What do you believe?

It is true that a person is appointed once to be born and once to die in the natural realm of life. But until the day that God has planned our earthly departure, let us follow the Word of God and pray the prayer of faith. We must never give up. As long as there is life, there is hope. Let us open ourselves to believe in the possibilities of miracles.

A miracle is a supernatural event that cannot be explained by human understanding, such as a physical healing. Miracles are the product of prayer and faith, a faith that chooses to believe in the supernatural promises of God.

Miracles happen in many different ways. Sometimes dreams and visions are used by God to reveal messages of instruction, warning, prophecy, comfort and confirmation. Sometimes revelations made way for the miracles of salvation, healing, protection or deliverance. In other instances miracles were the result of prayer and perseverance. Some miracles occur through the ministry of the gifts of the Holy Spirit. The chapter entitled "Why I believe in the Holy Spirit" will give to you more information about the various facets of the Holy Spirit and its workings.

Miracles can happen instantly or gradually over a period of time. On each page, you will see that miracles can happen any time, any place and in God's way. God may use people or sometimes angels to bring about a miracle.

In God's divine, unreachable wisdom, He created human beings, as an entity consisting of three components, the body which is the physical part of man; the mind which is the emotional part of man; and the spirit, which is the God consciousness part of man.

Are you hurting in body, mind or spirit? Take courage and don't give up. For many a despairing soul held on and struggled through the mountain and received their healing miracle on the other side.

This book is a collection of testimonials confirming the Word of God through signs, wonders and miracles. The miracles are broken down into three parts: body, mind and spirit. Throughout the book there are transforming miracles of salvation, miracles of physical healing, miracles of deliverance, miracles of protection and miracles of provision.

The purpose of this book is to encourage others to believe God for their miracle. Among the many miracles that I have shared are some of my own personal ones. I was at death's door several times, but God interrupted the shuttle of death, turned it around and kept me alive.

Do not read this book as just another book of someone's life experiences. But see the Living Word of God in action. As you read about the miracles in my life and the lives of others, may you be inspired to believe in God through faith to receive your miracle. There is so much more that God wants to do for us. Can you look beyond your situation and know that nothing is impossible with God? As you receive your miracle, may God empower you to help others believe for their miracle.

Have you ever invited the master of miracles, Jesus the Son of God into your heart? I have news for you! The greatest miracle of all miracles is the salvation of the soul. If you are open to accept Christ into your life, just repeat the following *Sinner's Prayer* and find yourself a good Bible believing church:

> *Jesus, I believe in my heart that you are the Son of God, and that you died on the cross for all my sins. I repent and I ask forgiveness for all of my sins and I want to be born again. I invite you into my heart and life as Lord and Savior. Thank you God for my miracle of salvation, the gift of eternal life, in Jesus Name, Amen!*

PART I

The

Body

(PHYSICAL)

"Who forgiveth all thine iniquities; who healeth all thy diseases;"
(Psalm 103:3)

"And we know that all things work together for good
to them that love God, to them who are the called
according to his purpose."
(Romans 8:28)

Chapter One

MIRACLES OF HEALING

He Sent Angels

It was December of 1972. The holidays were soon approaching. The air was filled with the Christmas spirit. At church we were always busy around this special holiday season. It was a time when we would invite families and the unsaved to hear God's Word demonstrated through a Christmas cantata and a salvation play portraying the Love of God.

At home this was a busy time of the year for me. Besides teaching in high school and being active in church work, I made time to bake cookies and bread, creating a warm atmosphere of the Christmas spirit in our home. Like everyone else, I would be shopping and buying gifts, not for myself, but for the needy and for our children.

As usual, we celebrated Christmas at home with our daughter and family who lived two hours away from us. But this year our plans changed. We decided to spend the holiday with our son and family who had recently moved to Long Island.

I did not want to leave Buffalo without seeing my daughter and her family. So we arranged to meet each other in Holland, New York, the halfway meeting place.

After I arrived home from teaching that afternoon, my son John and I packed the car with gifts and homemade cookies. We also decided to bring my daughter a beautiful blue spruce Christmas tree. It barely fit in the trunk of the car.

It was about 4:30 in the afternoon when we started on our trip. We were driving a new Chevrolet Impala. As far as we knew, everything was fine with the car.

Our meeting place was about 45 minutes away from home. We were on the road for about 25 minutes when I felt the car pulling toward the right side of the road. I slowed down for a little while, but as I picked up speed again, going 45 miles per hour, the car went totally out of control. The steering wheel was going in one direction and the wheels were going in the opposite direction.

There was a 75-foot drop on the right side of this main four-lane highway. My car was headed for that drop when suddenly it hit a reflector post that stopped the car from going down the 75-foot drop. The impact was so strong. It felt like I hit a Mack truck.

Knowing I had no control of the car, fear gripped my heart. All I could envision was a picture of the car going up in flames and our bodies burning. I wasn't concerned about myself, but for my son. Seeing this horrible image in my mind, I called out to God, *"Oh, God, please deliver us. If we come out of this car alive, I thank you for a miracle."*

With the impact of hitting the reflector post, my son woke up, screaming, "Mom, Mom, What is happening?"

"Don't worry Johnny, we'll be okay."

I had already prayed. It was all in the hands of the Lord.

After the car hit the reflector post, it was as though someone pushed it into the opposite direction. It crossed over the two one-way lanes and started to go up the six-foot high hilly and rocky divider that separated the four-lane highway. While this was happening, my son and I were bouncing in all directions, and I began to experience pain.

All of a sudden, I heard a voice commanding two angels to go to the right side of the car. They were taller than the car, floating with ease, obeying God's command. One was positioned at the front right side of the car and the other angel was positioned at the back right side of the car. Then I heard the Lord softly say, *"Let it go down easy, easy, easy."* Each time the word easy was spoken, the angels would stop for a second before the next word easy was spoken.

That was the sensation my son and I felt as the car came to a halt, lying down on its right side. The engine was still running and the car was smoking. We were told later that people wanted to help us, but they were afraid of the car igniting. By this time I had some injuries, but I was still conscious of everything that was happening. I heard a voice again, but this time it came like thunder. It was loud and forceful. *"Shut the ignition! Shut the ignition!"* I heard the voice, but I could not find the ignition because of my body's position. Someone pushed my hand directly on the ignition. It had to be the Lord because I felt the push, but I don't remember shutting the ignition off.

As soon as the car stopped smoking, two men came to take us out of the car. They first pulled my son John out through the car window. When the man saw how badly I was injured, he said, "Please, Miss, don't move and don't talk; just be still." I could barely whisper, but I told him I was just thanking God for the miracle. He pulled out a handkerchief and wiped the tears away from his face. I believe he was moved with tears recognizing that this was a miracle.

As they carefully pulled me out of the car through the window, I was concerned about the damages to the car, but the Lord would not allow me to look at them. It seemed as though I was only able to look upward to the sky, and as I did, I heard a soft soothing voice say, *"This is a new day in your life! This is a new day in your life!"*

After hearing those words, my focus in life took on a whole new meaning. The worry I had about the car's damages disappeared. Just before the accident I was in the middle of creating an official plaque for the college. It was to be one of my original photo designs with a photograph of the college. These plaques were to be given to noted personalities. With this work of art I would have been on my way to becoming a national artist. But after the accident, all the desire to complete this project had vanished.

All I could see before me were people dying, going to a Christ-less grave because they had not been told of the saving grace of Jesus Christ. This was all I could think about.

Among the spectators, there was a State Trooper who was called to the scene of the accident. After viewing the scene, he phoned my husband and said, "Mr. Franco, your wife was in a car accident. She is injured, but your son is okay. The car went totally out of control. We can't understand how the car did not go down the 75-foot drop!" Then he repeated it again, "I don't think you understood what I said. The car with your son and wife was headed for that 75-foot drop, but somehow the car turned and went in the opposite direction just before it was ready to down the drop. We don't know how that happened. You are fortunate to have your son and wife alive!"

I did not realize until several months later that a miracle had taken place at that point. As a guest on a television show called, "Health and Happiness," I was asked to share this testimony. While I was relating the incident of the reflector post I said, "It felt like I hit a Mack truck," and immediately, I heard in my spirit, *"Don't you know it was my hand that stopped the car from going down the 75-foot drop?"* Wow, what an awakening!

Later, we went back and examined the reflector post. There wasn't even a scratch on it. The State Trooper and the untouched reflector post confirmed that someone else stopped the car from going down the 75-foot drop. It was none other than the protective hand of God!

An ambulance was called to take me to the hospital. They took x-rays, but because of the internal bleeding my injuries did not show up on the x-rays. They said, "Sorry, we cannot keep her here at this hospital. We have to send her home because her doctor is not affiliated with us."

At home, I was weak and dizzy from passing blood. I thought to myself, "How could they send me home in this condition? What if I bleed to death?" But the words that I had heard at the accident scene, *"This is a new day in your life"* kept repeating in my mind and gave me some hope.

I had much suffering and pain following the accident. My son, John came out of the accident with only a little bruise on his shoulder. I began having seizures. My right leg had muscle and nerve damage.

The leg would not move voluntarily, but needed help. It also had become two inches longer than my left leg.

Again I found myself saying, "Lord, you said this is a new day in my life, but how can I serve you and my family in this condition? Did you spare my life so I would die later? I am confused, Lord. I don't understand why I am not being healed. Please, Lord speak to me. I need to hear from you."

Three months later, I was still suffering and seeing a doctor for medical treatment. The doctor observing that my right leg was not getting any better and it had started to drag said, "There is only one more type of treatment I can give you, and if this does not work, you will be—uh-" and he hesitated.

I responded, "Doctor, you mean I will be crippled?"

He put his head down and said, "Yes, Rose."

The doctor proceeded with the treatment. He injected 25 vials of medication in different areas of my right hip area. When he completed the treatment he said, "This medication should work within two weeks and if there is no change—uh-" again he hesitated.

Knowing what he was about to say I said to myself, "I will not be a cripple!"

Yes, the two weeks went by and there was no change. If anything, the condition had worsened. I went back to the doctor and he confirmed that the treatment did not work.

He said, "There isn't anything more that I can do for you, but see me in two weeks and maybe we can have another specialist see you."

First Healing Miracle after the Accident

I told myself, "Where do I go from here?" I knew I had to turn to my God for answers. He spared my life in that car accident. I was so desperate to hear from God. I told my husband I was going to church to pray. There were chores that I had to do at home and he said, "Why can't you pray at home?"

"No, I'm sorry John, but I need to hear from God. At church there will be no distractions."

I didn't want to be alone at the church, so I invited Mrs. Moore to pray with me. At the church, we were sitting in the first row, about eight seats away from each other. I was facing the front of the church. There was a painting of Jesus on the wall. Mrs. Moore started to pray a wonderful prayer before the Lord. I was so hungry to hear from God, that I looked at that painting of Jesus and prayed, "Lord, I know you are not here hanging on the wall. I know you are alive and living inside of me, but Lord, please heal me or take me home to be with you."

As I was sitting in the pew, I felt as though my body was lifted off the chair but in actuality my body did not move. Instead something was happening inside of me. I said, "Lord, if I can feel your presence in such a wonderful and powerful way, what is it for you to heal my leg?"

As I said this, I heard, "*If you only knew how much I love you.*"

Then I felt a hand touch my leg from my toes up to my hip. I heard several crackling sounds. I knew something had happened, but I didn't want to be disappointed. Gradually, I opened my eyes and called out to Mrs. Moore, "Mrs. Moore, look; my leg is healed!" I stretched both legs out and they were the same size. Praise the Lord! We both began thanking God for the miracle.

I kept my scheduled appointment with my doctor. At first I did not tell him about the healing. I was sitting on the table, and as usual he stretched out both of my legs and said, "This can't be; no, this can't be!" I said nothing. He washed his hands and left the room all confused. For a moment I thought he wasn't coming back, but within minutes he returned.

When he entered the room, I looked at him and smiled, "Doctor, do you want to know what really happened?"

He sat on the stool next to me and said, "Yes, Rose, I want you to tell me word for word just what happened."

After I shared God's divine miracle with him, he put his hand on my leg and with teary eyes he said, "Rose, don't ever lose that faith in God. This is a miracle." I never saw the doctor again.

Second Miracle after the Accident

When we had prayed at the church, I had only asked God to heal my leg. I don't know why I had not asked Him to heal me of the seizures, too. Whenever I had a seizure, I could hear everything that people were saying around me, but I could not speak or move any part of my body. The lower half of my body from the waist down would start shaking uncontrollably. This would last for about 20 minutes. When it was over, my mind would not close down. I couldn't sleep for several days. It was a horrible experience.

One day I was to speak at a young people's service and minutes before the service started, I had one of these attacks. People around me began praying, asking me to move my fingers. My mind got the message, but my nervous system was not responding.

It seemed that the seizure attacks were coming more frequently. I had a very bad one at home that caused me to lost my vision and speech for about 30 minutes. When my vision was gone, I thought, "Lord, you must be coming to take me home, I'm ready."

The paramedics were called to my home. One of the paramedics, seeing my condition, bent down close to my face and with compassion and tears in his eyes whispered, "We will not leave until you are feeling better." As he said this, a peace came over me. I felt he was another angel God had sent to comfort me. Later, the paramedic turned to my husband and said, "You had better get your wife to the best physician in town. If she gets another seizure as bad as this one, I'm afraid you will lose your wife."

Little did I know that a second miracle was on its way. John made an appointment for me to see a specialist. The doctor reviewed my case. He knew that John was recuperating from cancer surgery. The doctor suggested to my husband, "Get her away from your illness. Wherever you send her, she must be rushed to the hospital if she has another seizure."

Lillian, a woman from our church, was going to visit her husband who was working in Phoenix, Arizona. I had a sister living in Phoenix who loved the Lord. She always prayed with unwavering faith. My husband felt that it would be a good place to send me. This truly had to be God's timing.

He asked Lillian, "Would you mind if my wife travels with you to Phoenix?"

"I'd be thrilled to have my pastor's wife come with me."

The best is yet to come. My sister and her four daughters met me at the airport. They were so happy to see me, thinking that I was there for a vacation. They had made plans for me to go sightseeing with them. My sister had no previous knowledge of my illness. The first day I did not want to alarm her about my condition. I wanted to enjoy their fellowship.

I knew I couldn't put it off any longer. On the second day I told her about the seizures and what could happen if I should get one. I told her, "If I get a seizure, I will lose my speech. I have to be rushed to a hospital right away because I will need oxygen."

When I told her this, she wasn't alarmed at all. She went on to say, "You just need a good steak and some spinach. You'll be alright."

I thought to myself, "If she only knew what really happens, she wouldn't be talking that way." For a moment, I wondered if she understood what I had said. Questions began invading my mind, "Did I come to the right place? What will happen to me now if I get a seizure? Will they call an ambulance to rush me to a hospital?"

Later that day, I was sitting at her kitchen table peeling carrots. Suddenly, I felt a seizure coming on. As usual it started with a burning sensation radiating from my right arm. I told my sister, "Please, get me to a couch. I'm getting a seizure. Please hurry. Call an ambulance. Get me to a hospital!" Within minutes I became weak, and I couldn't walk or talk. It took all five of them to carry me onto the couch. When they saw what was happening to me, they became alarmed and concerned, but they did not allow fear to take over; instead, they put their trust and faith in the Lord.

As I was lying on the couch, my body from the waist down was shaking uncontrollably. My sister and her four daughters began to pray, rebuking the illness in the Name of Jesus, claiming healing for my body. Even though I was unable to speak, I could hear their prayers and supplication sent to the throne of God. As they were praying, within my mind and my spirit I was calling out to God, *"Lord, you have to honor their simple childlike faith."*

Every other time when I had a seizure, I would be wide-awake, but this time something happened. I went into a deep sleep, from five in the afternoon until two in the morning. When I awoke, my sister and her daughters were still all around me, some were praying and the others were sleeping.

God heard their sincere childlike faith and healed me completely from those dreadful seizures that were caused by the car accident. Thank God that was the last seizure that I experienced.

Through faith and prayer God brought these two healing miracles into my life. If a mustard seed of Faith can move a mountain, then how much faith do we need to receive a miracle?

Every day has been a new day in my life since the accident. My love and focus have turned completely to the Lord and His work. I find myself witnessing to the lost no matter where I am. Every day I live, I live for the Lord. I want my life to count for Him and I want to be available for His service in whatever way He chooses to use me. I owe my life to Him. There is no better satisfaction and joy then serving our Lord and Master.

God works in mysterious ways his wonders to perform. My son and I are alive today because my God sent His angels to deliver us from death. "For he shall give his angels charge over thee, to keep thee in all thy ways." (Psalm 91:11).

Where Two Can Agree

As part of my husband's ministry, one of his responsibilities was to make hospital calls to our members. One morning he called me from his office and asked me to make his hospital calls.

We had met a woman through her missionary stepdaughter. We had the privilege of introducing her to the Lord. One of the hospital calls was to visit this woman who had had surgery several days prior.

The woman's son, a heart surgeon told my husband, that his mother's doctor discovered that her body was full of cancer. They closed her incision and gave the family the sad news that there was nothing more they could do for her. They advised the family that she did not have long to live. The family did not tell their mother about her fatal condition. We were told to keep this diagnosis confidential and share it with no one else.

I called my coworker and prayer partner, Mrs. Moore, to join me in making the hospital visit. As we were driving to the hospital, Mrs. Moore began to pray that God would go before us and prepare our hearts for whatever was to take place during our visit. She also prayed that we might be used as instruments, led by the Holy Spirit, to bring honor and glory to His name.

We arrived at the hospital, and as we entered the woman's private room, our hearts went out to her. Prior to her illness, she had the most beautiful natural rosy complexion. But now her skin tone was a pale, chalky, grayish white. Her body was weak and frail--a typical appearance that death was eminent.

As we looked at her condition, we were overcome with love and compassion. At that moment, the faith of a mustard seed became a reality. It brought hope, where there was no hope. It brought life, where there seemed to be no life. As we moved in the realm of faith, it empowered us to believe and act upon God's Word. "Again I say unto you, that if two of you shall agree on earth as touching anything that they shall ask, it shall be done for them of my Father which is in heaven. For where two or three are gathered together in my name, there am I in the midst of them." (Matthew 18:19-20).

The room was filled with the divine presence of the Lord. Just before we began praying for our dear sister in Christ, she began to cry, as she directed our attention to a glass of milk. "I am so sick, I can't even drink milk or eat anything. Please pray for me."

We began by singing an Italian hymn that was dear to her heart, entitled, "Come, My Heart Is Calling For Thee, Oh Lord," as she wept before the Lord. I began to tell her, "Jesus loves you and is touched by your sufferings. Jesus himself suffered pain on the cross. And through His suffering and pain He bore our sickness. He made it possible for us through faith to receive healing for our bodies. He is our great physician and healer, let's believe and unite our hearts as we lift up His Name in prayer."

In one mind and one accord, we began praying for a miracle. Together, Mrs. Moore and I laid our hands on the woman's stomach area, as we claimed the promises of God by faith according to the scriptures.

The prayer was short and simple. *"Our heavenly Father, we come to you in the Name of Jesus, Your son, and in the power of the Holy Spirit. Unite our hearts as one. By faith we believe and claim the promises according to thy Word. We ask you to restore and renew every organ, every cell and tissue in her body. We come against this infirmity in the name of Jesus your Son; perform a miracle in her life to bring honor and glory to your name, Amen."*

Then Mrs. Moore followed with a fervent prayer that ended with, *"In Jesus Name we pray and believe it as done. Amen and Amen!"*

As we concluded the prayer and opened our eyes, we could hardly believe what we were witnessing! As we looked at the woman's hands, a very obvious change was taking place. The change started at her fingers, went up her arms, neck and into her face. Her skin changed from a chalky, grayish, white tone to her former lovely rosy complexion. What an instant healing!

When we saw this happening, I grabbed a mirror from my purse to show the dear sister the miracle that God had just brought into her life. She began saying. "I love you Jesus. I thank you, Jesus!" The instant visible change happened before our eyes, from her fingers all the way up to her face. What an unforgettable instant miracle! We marvel because we forget that Jesus raised people from the dead. He told us, that we would do greater things in His Name after we have received the infilling of the Holy Spirit.

This dear sister in Christ was not expected to leave the hospital alive, but God had a different plan for her life. After the Lord healed her, the doctor released her from the hospital and sent her to a senior complex.

A week later we visited her at the complex. She had gone from not being able to drink even a glass of milk, to eating a full course dinner. We could not help but rejoice with her for the miracle of healing that extended her life.

We did not see the woman's son, the doctor, until about a year later when his brother-in-law, a missionary, was scheduled to speak at our church. We invited the doctor, a non-believer, to attend the service. He was unable to make it, but he invited the young people's group and us to his luxurious home for refreshments and fellowship after the service.

His house was very large and beautiful. All together, there were over forty people at his home. The doctor had also invited several business friends and fellow doctors.

Everyone was busy socializing. Some were outside near the pool area, while others were in the large entertainment room. The doctor came to where I was sitting just off the entertainment room. He graciously greeted me and pulled up a chair next to me. As we were conversing, I questioned him about his mother, "Doctor, what did your mother's physicians attribute to her healing and well-being?"

He hesitated and then said, "Well, you know my mother's body was full of cancer. The doctor closed her incision and said, 'She won't make it; its just a matter of time. We'll do all we can to make her comfortable.' When they saw the change in her, they couldn't understand what had happened. The only answer they had for us was, 'All the cancer is gone. We believe she probably wanted to get well so badly that she willed herself to get well and recovered.'"

After hearing what the doctors had attributed to her healing, I could barely wait to tell him what happened the day we visited his mother in the hospital. "Doctor, do you want to know what really happened?"

He pulled up the chair even closer and said, "Please Rose, tell me everything!"

I shared with him in detail how the Lord divinely visited and healed his mother as we prayed with her. The doctor grabbed my hand and started to cry and said, "I knew there had to be more to her recovery. It had to be a miracle! Rose, please come with me. I want to gather everyone together and say a Prayer of Thanksgiving to God for my mother's miracle."

He gathered us all together in the large entertainment room and had us hold hands and form a circle. Then he asked his brother-in law, the missionary and my husband to offer prayers unto the Lord. What an opportunity to share the miracles of salvation and healing to the unsaved that were among us.

This incident began with a hospital visit, where two people agreed in prayer, according to Matthew 18:19,20, and together dared to believe that God could bring healing to a dying woman.

I believe, and have made it a practice, that when possible, it is always best to go two by two when making any type of a visit where prayer is needed. I have found through experience that while one is praying, the other person should be in agreement, backing them up in prayer. When we do this, we are obeying the teachings of Jesus.

Faith of a Child

Eleven months after we were married, the Lord blessed us with a set of twins, Robert Peter and Maria Linda. They brought much joy into our lives. We could not afford the conveniences that would make life a little easier for the twins or for ourselves: such things as individual cribs, double carriages and walkers.

The twins had to sleep together in one crib. One of them slept at the head of the crib and the other one slept at the foot of the crib. That wasn't too bad, except for one problem. For the first nine months Robert was awake during the night. He slept during the daytime while Maria slept during the nighttime. Due to Robert's abnormal sleep pattern, I went endless nights without sleep. But the joy of having a boy and a girl as our first born outweighed all the extra work, loss of sleep and inconveniences.

After potty training, we noticed that Robert had some difficulty with his bowel movements. At first, thinking it was a constipation problem, we didn't make much of it. But as time went on, we realized that it was something more serious. Robert would go three or four days without a bowel movement. When he had one, he would experience pain.

We made an appointment to see a doctor about this problem. The doctor was very concerned and immediately sent our son for x-rays. After reading the x-rays, he called us into his office. He waited for awhile, probably thinking, "How can I break this sad unusual finding to these people?" Finally, he broke his silence and said, "The x-ray findings were not very good. Your son has a rare and serious medical condition. He has an abnormal bowel tract. Instead of a normal single "S" bowel intestine, he was born with a double "S" bowel intestine."

The doctor prescribed a liquid medication for our son. We followed the instruction faithfully, hoping it would correct the problem. To our disappointment, there was no change in his bowel movements. The condition had become worse.

When we went back to the doctor we asked him if there was anything more he could do for our son. He suggested, "I'm afraid there isn't anything left to do, but surgery. This is a rare physical condition. There are only two doctors (at that time) who are able to perform this type of surgery. One is in Canada, and the other one is in Europe. I must tell you, there is no guarantee that this type of surgery will be successful. This is a very serious surgery and the success rate is very low."

We left the doctor's office broken-hearted over the medical report of our son's rare physical condition. Due to this problem sometimes he would hide behind the couch because of pain and shame. Seeing him suffer with this condition was so painful for me. Knowing he would have to start school soon gave me great concern.

I am sure there are many parents who have asked the same questions as I did. *"Why, Lord, why my child Lord? What did I do Lord to deserve this?"* When we are faced with the heartache of seeing a child suffer with an abnormal affliction or any serious sickness, it is almost impossible not to become a victim of such questioning.

My husband and I went before the Lord in intercessory prayer, *"Lord, what do we do now? You heard the slim hope the doctor gave us. If Robert has the surgery, there's no guarantee that it will be successful. We just don't know what to do. Lord, we ask for guidance, knowing that your wisdom surpasses the limited knowledge of humans. We put our son in your hands. You have the power to restore and to recreate. We ask you, our great physician, to heal our child whom you have given to us; in Jesus Name we pray and believe it!"*

After praying we felt that God heard our prayer even though there was no physical evidence of my son's healing. Little did we know what God had in store. In a few days things were about to change.

While we were at a church service, Jim, a church member, told us he was going to take his son to a healing service. His son suffered with asthma. Jim heard about our son's medical condition and invited us to go with him. The healing service was to be held in New York City with Evangelist William Branham.

As of that time, I had never been to a mass healing service. I was in my 20s and had had little exposure to God's healing power. But I was desperate. I was not concerned as to where the healing would take place. I just wanted God to heal my son no matter where or how.

When I told my husband I was going to the healing service, he said, "Why do you have to go to New York City for our son to be healed? God can heal him here."

"John, I agree with you. But, for some reason, I have this feeling that we should go."

Reluctantly, he said, "Well, that is my feeling about going, but if you feel you should go, that's fine."

I wanted to please my husband, but I knew in my heart that I had to go. The Lord had spoken to me not to my husband. It was my responsibility to be steadfast and follow the leading of the Holy Spirit; even if this means standing alone.

Before we knew it, we were off to the healing service with Brother Jim and his son. My son and I sat in the back seat of the car. We prayed as we traveled to the service. We arrived at Carnegie Hall where the service was being held. The only seats available were up in the balcony. As we were seated there, Brother Jim went downstairs to get some prayer cards. While he was gone, my son was silently praying to the Lord for his healing. After praying, he looked at me and said, "Mom, God can heal me right here." I believe that God honored the faith of this little child and started the healing process right there in the balcony.

While Brother Jim was getting the prayer cards, he managed to get four seats in the second row from the platform. At first my son was hesitant about moving, but eventually we made our way down to the second row.

A crippled teenage boy was sitting in the seat next to my son. The service started with a song about the healing power of God. The speaker, Brother Branham, humbly approached the podium. He appeared as one who had just been in the presence of God. There was an aura of holiness around him.

He had a Word of Knowledge for several people in the audience when suddenly the anointing of the Holy Spirit so overwhelmed him that he could barely stand up. He told the people, *"God's healing power is so strong in this building. If you need a touch from God, stand to your feet and receive your healing."* There were people standing up all over the building.

I can never forget how the young boy next to my son stood up and threw his crutches away and began thanking God for this instant healing. This was quite an inspiration for my son. When he saw this happen, he raised his hands toward heaven and began thanking God for his own healing.

What an incredible blessing was experienced by many as the Holy Spirit permeated the auditorium, causing a mass healing to take place. There was no laying on of hands, just a divine visitation of God's healing power.

I knew my son was healed, even though the evidence was not yet visible. As we were traveling back home, Robert looked at me with a big smile and said, *"Mommy, I know God healed me tonight. I don't know if Daddy will believe me, but I know that I am healed."* These are the words spoken by a four-year-old child!

I cannot help but think of the scripture that says, "Whosoever shall not receive the kingdom of God as a little child shall in no wise enter therein." (Luke 18:17). Let us exercise the faith of a little child so that we can receive all God has for us.

The evidence of my son's healing began to show the very next day. He started having loose bowel movements for three days. God was performing an internal surgery without the intervention of man. After the three days he moved his bowels every other day. About a week later and every day following, our son had a normal movement. Only God could perform such a wonderful miracle. To God be the glory.

We went back to the doctor and told him what had happened. We shared how a four-year-old child had faith in God for his healing. The doctor looked at us in amazement and said, "I have never heard of anything like this happening; it can only be what they call a miracle!"

Oh that our prayer may be, *"God grant us simple childlike faith. May our hearts be pure in thy sight, and may we walk in faith, believing and expecting our miracle."*

Looking Beyond

It was a very busy season for me. I was teaching Art and Photography in high school, enrolled in a master's program at SUNY and advisor to the Young Adult's Department in our church. In the midst of this busy schedule I received a call from Long Island, New York, that my dad had become critically ill. He was in a nursing home and had to be rushed to a hospital. His condition was severe. He was given only a five to ten percent chance of living.

I discussed with my husband about visiting Dad. He quickly replied, "Why don't you wait, because if he is that critical, it would mean another trip later." I realized that our finances were limited, having two children in college plus my schooling expenses. Rather than responding to my husband's advice, I decided to pray before making a decision.

Proverbs 3:6, "In all of your ways acknowledge him and he shall direct thy paths," kept coming before me. I knew what I had to do. I had to go on my knees and include the Lord in my decision. As I prayed, I felt strongly that I was to go and be with my dad. I asked the Lord to give me a sign so my husband would be at peace knowing it was God's will for me to go.

In the meantime, I began calling the airlines about the cost of a round trip ticket from Buffalo to Long Island. Unbeknown to me, the young people from our church, together with my assistant director, Mrs. Moore, were led to take up an offering for me. No one in the group including Mrs. Moore knew anything about my conversation with my husband. They only knew that my dad was very sick.

On Wednesday night, after the youth service, Mrs. Moore handed me a little brown bag and said, "Mrs. Franco, if you want to visit your dad, the young people collected this money to help toward your trip." All I could think about was how I had asked the Lord for a sign. I had no idea of how much money was in the brown bag.

I turned around to Mrs. Moore and asked her to please wait while I counted the money. She helped me count the quarters, dimes, nickels, pennies and dollar bills. When we added it all up, I was speechless to discover that the cost for my round trip ticket, right to the last penny was in that little brown bag.

I shared this little miracle of provision with my husband about how God supplied the money to pay for my round trip. He looked at me and said, "What can I say, except that the Lord must want you to go visit your dad." Knowing that the young people did not have much money, we realized this could not be a coincidence. It was God's sign for me to go.

Without wasting any time, I got the first available flight. I arrived in Long Island on Sunday. My sister met me at the airport. The next morning on her way to school, she left me off at the hospital. I had planned to stay in Long Island until Friday. I brought some textbooks with me, planning to do some reading during the long hours at the hospital.

As I entered my dad's room, I placed the books on the windowsill. All the time I was at the hospital, I never once opened the books. Instead, I felt a strong need to pray and keep my mind on the Lord.

As I looked at my dad, seeing his frail condition, my human instinct told me, "There is no hope. He will not make it." To see my dad, a handsome, six-foot-tall man, who took pride in his appearance, now lying in bed, full of bedsores, all curled up and facing the wall was shocking and painful to me. He also had lost a lot of weight. I knew he felt badly that I had to see him in that condition.

I called out to my dad, "Papa, I'm Rosina, your daughter. I came from Buffalo to be with you." He nodded his head to acknowledge me, but he did not turn around to face me. I began to pray quietly for him. As I was praying, the Holy Spirit in a soft but firm voice said, *"Look not upon what you see, but look beyond."*

With these profound words, I began to act upon them, dismissing the carnal thinking that invaded my mind when I first entered the room. I realized that by looking at the circumstances, I could never envision a healing for my dad. I had to apply the Word of God by faith believing for the healing virtue of Jesus Christ to go beyond the sickness. *What seems impossible to man is possible with God, if we can only believe and act upon it.*

I was reading a tract on salvation when my dad's attending doctor came into the room. He politely asked me to leave. After he examined my dad, he turned to me and said, "Who are you?"

"Doctor, that man lying in bed is my dad. I am his daughter from Buffalo, New York."

The doctor reluctantly told me that my dad only had a five to ten percent chance of living. He said, "Your father's medical condition is very serious. He has no control of his bladder. He also has a blockage in his intestines."

I thanked him for the medical information and said, "I believed that God, who created my dad's body, could also heal him."

He looked strangely at me and said, "Well, I want you to know there is no hope."

"I understand what you said, but please, doctor, read this tract. After reading it, you will understand why I believe that my dad can be healed. It will also introduce you to Jesus Christ, the Son of God, who gave His life in exchange for us to have the gift of eternal life."

I will never forget the expression on the doctor's face. At first, he refused the tract and said, "I don't have any time to read it."

"Doctor, it is almost twelve noon. Are you going to stop for lunch?"

"Yes."

"Why would you take time out for lunch?" I replied.

"I need to feed my body to keep it healthy."

"Doctor, we are made up of body, mind and spirit. We take good care of the physical and mental parts of our being, but we make no time to nurture the spiritual part of our being. When God created man, He breathed His breath in man and made him a living soul. To become a healthy, whole person that God intended for us, we need to grow and mature in the three areas of our lives. You can only experience the fullness of life when Jesus Christ, the Son of God, comes and lives within your heart. Please Doctor, take time to read this tract. It will help prepare you for eternity."

In sharing this simple truth, the Holy Spirit was at work. Little tears were coming down his cheeks from behind his sunglasses. Then he put his hand out and said, "I will take it and I will make time to read it." He thanked me for sharing.

After the doctor left the room, I went over to my dad's bedside. I was aware that the great physician, the Lord Jesus, was there with us. Our Lord had heard the earthly doctor's report. I was moved by the Holy Spirit to pray a simple prayer in faith believing for a miracle. I began repeating over and over, *"Lord, I claim your healing virtue over his body, from his head to his toes, in the Name of Jesus Christ of Nazareth."* This went on for several minutes.

I ended the prayer with, *"Lord, you said, 'Look not upon what you see, but look beyond.' I believe your Word. I am crossing beyond the line of what my human eyes are seeing to where there is hope and healing in you. I know Lord that nothing is impossible with you. I call on you, our great physician, to intervene and bring healing to my dad."*

One could not help but feel the presence of the Lord all over that room. Then again, I heard the soft still voice of the Holy Spirit saying, *"Remind your father of what I have done for you and your family through his life."*

I reminded him of the great expectations he had had for his children. In the secular world he had the capabilities and finances to make them happen. My mother told me how much he loved us, and about the big ideas he had for his girls. He would line us up along the wall and say, "One day my four girls will be singing on stage and on radio." He was a lover of music.

"Papa, knowing Jesus Christ is much greater then any earthy fame and fortune we might have had. You gave us the best gift ever when you introduced us to Jesus. We have a peace and joy that the world and all its fame cannot give us. All of us children and most of your grandchildren are now serving God in different ministries."

As I reminded him of his part in our salvation, he was breathing deeply and sighing. Tears were falling down his face. Then I heard the Holy Spirit say, *"With every sigh there cometh a healing."* I prayed with my dad and ended the prayer with, "God is good, Papa, and He loves you."

Then with the little strength he had, he whispered, "Yes, Amen."

Up to this time my dad was unable to eat. He could not take any medication by mouth. The nurse came into the room and tried to give him a white liquid medication, but he was unable to swallow it. The nurse seeing this left the room. Not long after she left, as I was quietly sitting down and praying, I asked my dad if he would like some Jell-O, and he immediately responded, "Yes. Please some Jell-O!"

I asked the nurse in charge if my dad could have some Jell-O. She replied, "No way! Your father cannot swallow anything because he has a blockage in his esophagus." I told her that I would take full responsibility. The nurse told me she would call his doctor and get back to me.

About 20 minutes later the nurse came into Dad's room with the Jell-O and said, "The doctor said to do whatever that woman tells you to do." This was the same doctor to whom I gave the tract on salvation. Can you see how God works? I often wondered what went through the doctor's mind when this nurse spoke to him. I am sure there had to be some conviction from the Lord for him to respond in that manner.

As I began feeding my dad the Jell-O, I repeated the words I heard in my spirit, *"With every spoonful in the Name of Jesus."* As I obeyed and followed the leading of the Holy Spirit, Dad had no problem swallowing the Jell-O. When he finished what was in the bowl, he asked me for more.

You can just imagine the look on the nurse's face when I asked her for more Jell-O. She was speechless and could not believe what was happening. She sent a second bowl up to the room. Again I obeyed the Lord and repeated, *"With every spoonful in the Name of Jesus."* Each spoonful went into his stomach and stayed down. Praise the Lord! I knew something had happened, even though the evidence had not fully manifested itself.

When the nurse called the doctor back and told him what had happened, he ordered a soft diet for my dad's dinner.

God wants our obedience, no matter how foolish it may sound to us. Scripture records such an account. We read in John 9:1-7 how the man who was blind from birth received his healing. Jesus could have healed the blind man by touching him or just speaking the word as He did in other healings, but instead He first anointed the man's eyes with clay; then He told the man, "Go, wash in the pool of Siloam." It wasn't until the blind man obeyed the command of Jesus that he had received his sight.

I knew what I had to do the next day. I had to obey the Holy Spirit and repeat the prayer before his breakfast. His meal stayed down and every other meal from then on stayed down. Each day they increased his food intake and began giving him regular meals.

I was scheduled to fly back to Buffalo on Friday. On Wednesday, I was surprised to learn that a colonoscopy procedure for my dad had been previously scheduled for that Saturday, before my arrival at the hospital. I knew in my heart that God had touched my dad, and so I did not want to see him suffer through this test if it was not needed.

In order for me to be present for this test, I had to extend my stay three extra days. It cost 20 dollars more to make the change. I called my husband to get his approval. He laughed and said, "You will not believe this. A woman came up to me after the service and gave me 20 dollars toward your trip." As I previously mentioned, my original ticket was fully paid by the young people. This 20 dollars covered the additional cost of changing my return trip. I believe this was in God's plan from the beginning.

Saturday morning came around much too soon for me. My sister and I were in the waiting room. The doctors had started the procedure.

As my sister sat there correcting school papers, I quietly began praying to the Lord, *"Please Lord, give me a sign. If my dad was healed, why does he have to go through this test? I ask you Lord to go into that operating room and direct those doctors."* About 45 minutes later, the doctors came out of the operating room and said, "We don't know what happened, but we cannot go through with this test."

I had all I could do to hold back from shouting, *"Thank you, Jesus for answering my prayer and for the sign reassuring me that you have healed my dad."* At that time I felt this answer to prayer was only for me to know. I did not share this with anyone, knowing others were not ready to receive the news of what God had done. There is a time when we need to be silent, wait and let the Lord show His glory in His way and in His timing. He knows the beginning from the end.

After I left my dad at the hospital, he returned to the nursing home and I did not hear from anyone about his condition. About two weeks after I had returned home to Buffalo, I called the nursing home to check on his condition. The supervising nurse, who was my relative, answered the phone. I asked her, "How is my dad doing?"

She said. "Just a minute, Rose," and she left the phone booth. I was surprised when I heard another person's voice instead of the supervisor. Yes, it was my dad, who only had a five to ten percent chance of living. When he greeted me my heart was overwhelmed with joy. We conversed for a few minutes thanking God for the miracle.

The nurse came back on the phone and said, "Rose, this is a miracle if I have ever seen one. Your father eats well. He also has full control of his bladder and his bowels. Yes, I must say this is a miracle."

The obstruction in his bowels and bladder never returned. When God does a work, the evidence will follow. God granted Dad 15 more years of life and he lived to age of 94. It is never too late for a miracle.

After reading this chapter, I trust you have seen how God worked out His plan to bring about the fulfillment of this miracle through obedience. Sometimes, the Lord will ask us to say or do something that seems like foolishness to our human understanding. But, no matter how foolish it may sound, all He wants from us is to trust and obey His leading. Besides performing a miracle, God also revealed the importance of obedience. It is the Lord who performs miracles through obedient, yielded vessels.

Remember the title "Looking Beyond" and apply it to your life. Never allow the circumstances to stop you from receiving your miracle.

Tears Turn to Joy

We were ready to take on our first full-time pastorate. My husband, John, was scheduled to be a candidate for a church in Youngstown, Ohio. My sister-in-law agreed to take care of our children, while we were away.

All preparations were made, and we were to leave for Ohio later that day. My sister-in-law came to our home bright and early and stayed with my children while I went to the beauty shop. I was away no longer than 45 minutes when the cashier called my name and said, "Rose, you have an urgent call from your sister-in-law."

I became alarmed. Immediately, I prayed to myself, "Oh Lord, I hope everything is okay."

I no sooner picked up the phone and barely said, "Hi!" when my sister-in-law in a very excitable voice said, "Rose, you must get home right away. Johnny Boy is crying uncontrollably and I do not know what is wrong with him. Please come home as quickly as you can."

I could not get home fast enough. My heart was beating rapidly. I took the back streets to save time. As I entered the door of my home, I knew immediately that my 15-month-old son was very ill. As I picked him up to comfort him, I noticed that he was experiencing pain on the left side of his little body. I checked his temperature and it was 104.5 degrees.

He had been sick with a virus several weeks before and his doctor had ordered an antibiotic. Two weeks later he had a reoccurrence of the virus. This time, the doctor prescribed a different antibiotic. This one seemed to help clear up the virus and he was doing well and back to his normal self.

Johnny Boy appeared to be fine that morning. There were no warning signs of any illness. This sudden unexpected illness caused us great concern. Changes had to be made in our plans. I decided to stay home and take care of my son. My husband did not know what to do about going to Youngstown. I told him, "John, you go and don't worry. We'll keep you informed."

Before he left, we prayed together. My in-laws hearing the sad news came to our home. Grandpa Franco went into Johnny Boy's bedroom. I heard him praying to the Lord, *"Oh, Lord, heal Johnny Boy. He is just an infant. If you have to take anyone, take me. I have lived my 70 years of life. Please spare his life, Lord."* God did call Grandpa Franco home unexpectedly in October of that year.

When I called the pediatrician, he told me, "Bring your son to the hospital as soon as possible and I will meet you there." I was at the hospital holding my son in my arms when the doctor arrived. Before he even ordered a bed for my son, he said, "I want to do a spinal tap on your son." A spinal tap on my 15-month-old child? I refused and kept my son cuddled in my arms.

Before Johnny Boy was born, I had worked in the business office at this hospital for the administrator. I had been aware of some of the unfavorable results that had occurred due to the spinal tap procedure. I did not want my son's body to be invaded with a fluid that could blind or cripple him for life. In this situation I strongly knew that I was not to have this procedure performed on my son. I am not advocating that someone else should make the same decision that I made.

I knew the medical staff would not go along with my decision. But I had to remain firm and follow my heart.

The administrator's secretary heard what was going on and very nicely tried to persuade me, "Rose, put your son down and go along with the doctor." I told her, "I'm sorry Mrs. B. I will not allow my son to have the spinal tap, but I will agree to a blood test. If the doctor agrees with my decision, then I will admit my son."

Again the doctor and Mrs. B tried to convince me, "You're not doing what is best for your son. How could you do this, Rose?" They did not persuade me. I knew I had to stand firm even though I did not fully understand why.

Don't overwork your brain trying to understand why the Holy Spirit directs us to say or do a certain thing. He knows the future and wants what is best for us. His Spirit will work through us to bring about His plan for our lives.

The results of the blood test were in. The doctor called me and asked me to have my husband take a blood test to see if he had any trace of Mediterranean Anemia. My husband's test was negative. I was also told that my son could possibly have spinal meningitis.

When my husband heard this, he asked the church in Youngstown to pray and seek God for our son's healing. He told the Lord, *"I am here doing your work. Please, Lord, go to my son's hospital room and put your healing hand upon his body."*

It was comforting to know their prayers were with us. But the burden of seeing my son so sick was too much for me to bear. He had no food intake for two days, and he had blood drawn from his neck and from his ankle area several times a day.

The hospital hematologist, whom I knew from working in the business office, saw me in the hall. He had read my son's blood test and the results were not good. His blood count was down to six, far below the normal range for his age. This doctor confided with me, "Due to the findings in the blood test, if your son is given a blood transfusion, there is a possibility that he could develop palsy or be paralyzed." When I heard this, my heart was broken. Without my husband by my side, I had to rely completely on the Lord.

As the hematologist was sharing this frightening news with me, the pediatrician and our family doctor were coming down the hallway to speak to me about my son. The first words that the pediatrician said as he approached me were, "Mrs. Franco, due to your son's low blood count, we have to give him a blood transfusion. We will start it this afternoon." I was speechless, as the hematologist stood by and heard what I was told and said nothing. I desperately wanted to tell the pediatrician what the hematologist had told me about the blood transfusion, but how could I break his confidence? I felt helpless and asked the Lord, "What can I say now? They will criticize my faith, thinking that I am against blood transfusions. Please, help me Lord!"

I started to say, "Can I call my husband before…."

At that point, the pediatrician interrupted me with a loud voice and said, "If you think for one minute that I am going to get a heart attack over your son, you are wrong!"

Our family doctor was with the pediatrician. Even though his brother was a minister, he was an atheist.

Until now, in our conversation with the pediatrician the family doctor had said nothing. He waited, and then with a grin and sarcastic look on his face, he said to the pediatrician, "It must be because of her religion that she refused to give her son the blood transfusion."

I immediately answered him, "No doctor. That is not the reason!" Then something from deep inside of me said, "It's okay. Tell him yes for the blood transfusion." I reluctantly gave my approval, but at the same time, I wondered if I did the right thing for my son.

I left the hospital crying. On my way home I stopped by my mother's home to unburden myself. Seeing how discouraged I was, she said, "Now, don't worry. God will take care of Johnny Boy. He belongs to the Lord and no harm will come to him. Let us believe God and stand on His promises. My daughter, let us pray together and trust God."

After praying I still was not fully convinced that I had done the right thing. I was faced with the question, "What if? Will I ever forgive myself?"

I could not wait until I arrived home. I threw myself at the foot of my bed. The tears were flowing uncontrollably. I cried out to God, *"Lord, I do not understand. My husband is doing your work and is not here to share this burden with me that weighs heavy on my heart. Lord, I have no release. I need your strength and comfort to pull me through this trial. Please Lord, you are the Great Physician. You have the power to heal the son that you have given to us."*

After pouring my heart out to God, something wonderful happened. All of a sudden, it felt like a flood of living water was flowing down from my head to my toes. Wow! The burden was lifted from me. I had the assurance that my son was going to be okay, and I no longer worried about the blood transfusion. I was inspired to go to the piano. As I sat at the piano, the Lord gave me a song for my son. *"Go to sleep my baby. Go to sleep my love. Sleep tight my baby, dream of heaven above. There will be no sorrow, just you wait and see. Sleep tight my baby, The Lord is watching thee."*

I went back to the hospital that afternoon, and I inquired at the desk about the blood transfusion. For some reason the doctors had delayed it until the next morning. I knew the Lord was in this change, so I was at peace about it.

I went to my son's room. He was crying because he was hungry. He had no food intake for two days. I began singing the song the Lord gave me, and he peacefully went to sleep. That same night the church and my husband were praying for our son's complete healing. I left the hospital at 11 p.m., and drove home rejoicing in the Lord.

The next morning I went back to the hospital, knowing God had intervened. I was told to wait in the lobby because it was too early to visit my son. While I was sitting there, the pediatrician came out of the conference room adjacent to the lobby with eight other doctors. As he started toward me, I asked him, "How is Johnny Boy doing?"

He quietly said, *"That is what I want to talk to you about. See all these doctors. We just had a conference to discuss your son's case because we cannot explain or understand what has happened. For three days we drew blood from him. We gave him no food and yet, his blood count went up to 14."*

Immediately I said, "Thank God!"

The doctor looked at me and said. "You had better thank God! We still gave him the transfusion to build him up. Rose, remember to bring him to my office once a month so we can check his blood count. You know, it could happen again."

All Glory be to our God who reigns on high! His spirit dwells among those who love Him and obey Him and put their trust in Him no matter what the cost. Our son's blood count was normal at each visit. Finally after a few months, the doctor said, "You don't have to come back any longer. Johnny Boy's blood count has not changed. This is a miracle if I have ever seen one!" When God gives a miracle, He doesn't take it back. Our son was totally healed of this blood condition. Praise God!

What a living testimony this was for our family doctor, an atheist. He was surprised about Johnny Boy's miracle. We believe it was a sign for him to know that there is a God who is alive and answers prayers. We noticed a change in his attitude. He demonstrated respect for our faith in God and began asking many questions about our religious beliefs.

When trials come your way, I pray that the Lord will turn your tears into joy as you put your faith and trust in him.

Prayer Partner's Healing Miracle

Several of the healing testimonies included in my book took place when my prayer partner, Mrs. Moore, and I were praying or visiting the sick. I thank God for her faithful life to the Lord and His work and most of all for her unwavering faith and belief in the supernatural workings of the Holy Spirit. We have remained prayer partners since we worked together with the youth at the Calvary Christian Church in Buffalo, New York. We have witnessed the moving of the Holy Spirit in our youth meetings, and we are happy to say that many of them are serving the Lord today.

Throughout the years, even though we are hundreds of miles away from each other, whenever there is a need for prayer, we communicated by telephone. The results are many answered prayers including some miracles. I believe the reason that God answered these prayers is because we both agree with the same measure of faith knowing that all things are possible with God. Individually, we both have experienced the miracle-working power of God in our own lives through healing and deliverance from death.

The key word is agree. I believe many times it is very hard to find someone who fully agrees with you in prayer. Several months ago, a dear friend called requesting prayer for her son who was sent to prison. I asked my friend if she approved of my prayer partner, Mrs. Moore, joining us in prayer by phone. She responded, "That would be wonderful." The three of us prayed in agreement for her son, asking God to save his soul. Within a few weeks I received a call from my friend that her son gave his heart to the Lord. Then she thanked me for our prayers and said, "Sister Franco, you are so blessed to have a prayer partner. I am so desirous for God to give me someone who has the same measure of faith to believe and agree with me in prayer."

My friend was right. I have been blessed to have Mrs. Moore as a godly prayer partner for over 30 years. If the Lord has given you a faithful, God-fearing prayer partner, you are blessed. How comforting and rewarding it is when you have someone you can pray with and freely talk to about any need. One who will not only agrees with you in prayer but who will also keep your confidence.

As I have shared my personal healing miracles, I would like to include Mrs. Moore's miraculously healing testimony. By understanding the magnitude of this incident, one can realize that it could only be the God of the impossible who healed Mrs. Moore both physically and spiritually. I trust that your faith will be inspired as you read this incredible testimony.

Miraculously Snatched from the Brink of Death
Written by Mrs. S. Moore

In the early hours of November 18, 1962, I fell from the International Railroad Bridge in Buffalo, New York, to the hard pavement of the thruway below. It was a distance of about 30 feet. My skull was fractured, and my jawbone had been thrust through to my brain, disfiguring me beyond recognition. The bones of my right leg were shattered, and my pelvis was broken with the fragments perforating my internal organs.

The doctors at Meyer Memorial Hospital gave my family very little hope for my recovery. In fact, they said that if I did live, I would be a "blithering idiot" because of the injury to the brain.

During those early days at the hospital I was in severe pain. I felt as though my life were ebbing away. I became very concerned about my spiritual condition.

Way back at the beginning of the long, long path to that drunken moment on the bridge, I had a precious Christian mother who taught me to love and have reverence for the Lord. But after she went to heaven, our family drifted apart from one another and from the things of God. My husband was a good man, and I had two lovely children, but God was left out of our home and our lives were empty. We tried to fill the emptiness with social drinking and drifted into a round of parties.

Now I found myself in a hopeless condition, pleading with the nurse for a visit from a minister. It seemed that he never came. Then with my last bit of strength I cried to the Lord and vowed if He would spare my life so that I could bring up my children, I would live for Him. I wept tears of repentance. And then it seemed I heard a voice reassuring me that my prayer had been heard.

Meanwhile a Christian neighbor had given the newspaper clipping of my accident to her pastor at the Christian Church. He came and pointed me to the way of salvation through Christ. He led me to full assurance and peace. Now I knew I was a child of God!

A team headed by a plastic surgeon and dental surgeon set my face back into shape by wiring me from eyes to chin. Later, a 10-inch metal plate replaced the fragmented bone in my leg. There was a four-inch metal pin in my hip.

The pastor regularly visited to encourage me in my Christian experience and brought gospels and other literature. I told him I would love to read these, but could not. (My vision was so dim I could not see the nurse in her white uniform if she were standing just outside the open door!) He encouraged me to believe that the Christ who gave sight to the blind could now restore my sight and enable me to read; he prayed to this end and left.

The following day the patient in the bed next to mine saw me pick up a paper and asked, "Are you looking at the pictures?"

I replied, "No, I'm reading!"

She almost jumped out of her bed, exclaiming, "I heard that minister pray that you would be able to read!" This definite demonstration of the Lord's power to heal helped to build up my faith for further victories.

After ten weeks in the hospital, I obtained reluctant permission to return home. Strict orders were given to never put my weight on the injured leg. I moved about in a wheelchair with that leg on a horizontal extension. As soon as I could, I began to attend church services on crutches. From time to time I suffered severe headaches, loss of hearing, and once even the loss of my voice - lingering effects of my fall from the bridge.

During my follow-up examinations, I kept asking the doctors whether they expected that I would ever walk again. They finally told me that, even after years of care, there was the likelihood that the 10-inch metal plate would not hold under pressure, in which case my leg would have to be amputated.

I could not accept this verdict. One night after my family had retired, I brought my grief to the Lord. As I wept before Him, it seemed that a mighty hand came down on my shoulder and I felt in my heart that God would undertake to heal me before very long!

About two months later an evangelist came to our church. He announced that on Friday evening, September 27, 1963, he would preach on divine healing and pray for the sick. I knew God's people were praying, but things were against me that day. I awoke with one of those severe headaches, also my leg was very sore around the metal plate and pin; but I was determined to believe God.

When we were invited to come forward for prayer, I came down the aisle on crutches. After I was prayed for, I returned to my seat, still using my crutches. But when I sat down God spoke to me, saying, "You are as whole as anyone in this room." With a cry of joy I threw my crutches away and walked home without them. The wheelchair was discarded, and I have walked unaided ever since. That night I was too excited to go to bed. Our lights were on until 3 a.m. as neighbors came to "congratulate" me on my healing. For days neighbors kept coming in to see the miracle for themselves!

At the next scheduled examination the doctors were amazed to see me putting my weight on the precarious leg and walking without crutches. They ordered new x-rays and seemed bewildered as they compared the new with the old.

From that time, thank God, I was able to care for my husband and children and do all my housework. A slight limp is about the only visible effect of the experience that brought me to the gates of death. But through it all my husband and children received the Lord Jesus as their personal Savior, and I became hungry for the baptism in the Holy Spirit. One evening as I completely yielded myself to the Lord, there came the manifestation of speaking in other tongues. Thank God for this more abundant life of joy and power. Both spiritually and physically the Lord has redeemed my life from destruction.

Truly the wages of sin is death. My own reckless, rebellious way had brought me to the very brink of hell. The worldly pleasures and allurements of sin cannot in any way be compared with the peace, joy and freedom that are now mine in Christ. By His grace I want to always live for Him.

Two Weeks to Live

In September of 2001 we left California, and we were anxiously looking forward to our New York trip. One of our former members had become the pastor of a growing church outside of Buffalo. My husband was invited as one of the speakers for the dedication of the new building.

While in New York, we stayed on a few extra days to visit with our daughter. Somewhere while eating, I contracted some bad bacteria. I began to feel sick, dizzy and had stomach pains with a bad case of diarrhea. At first I wasn't concerned. I started taking over-the-counter medication thinking it would go away in a few days. But instead the condition worsened, and I found myself in a hospital.

My body was dehydrating. Intravenously, they were replenishing the fluid in my body. Mrs. Moore, my prayer partner whose husband worked in that hospital, came and prayed on my behalf.

I was hospitalized in New York for four days. After being discharged, the condition still continued. I had a difficult time eating.

No matter what I ate, I would continue to have pain in my stomach and lower intestines. The diarrhea condition continued. My husband felt we should go back to California, but all flights were canceled because of 9-11. As soon as the ban on flights was lifted, we flew home.

The day after we arrived, I went to the doctor's office. He admitted me into the hospital for tests. While in the hospital my blood test showed that my white cell count was high. It was apparent that all the focus was on the white cell count, instead of the bad bacteria that was destroying my insides. I was moving my bowels ten to fifteen times a day, mostly liquids. Each day I became weaker and more dehydrated.

They brought in doctors with different medical specialties. I had at least eight doctors diagnosing my medical condition. Each one prescribed different medications and tests. They ordered every test imaginable. Some of these medications were administrated through the veins and others orally. I was given steroids that caused me to have high blood pressure, water retention and diabetes.

At one point, I was taking about 40 pills a day. I complained about being overmedicated, but the doctors insisted, telling my family that I had to take them in order to live. At one nursing home, a nurse openly told me that I was taking more pills per day than any other patient. You can't imagine what this did to me.

I never was a "pill popper." I have always been a believer in taking care of my body by eating balanced meals, taking vitamins, bike riding, swimming and walking. Most of all, because of my relationship with God, no matter what happened around me, I worked hard on keeping a joyous and positive attitude toward life. I led a very busy life, being available for my family's needs, ministering with my husband, and teaching or working part-time selling real estate to supplement our income.

In the beginning of my sickness I had lost a tremendous amount of weight. But later because of the steroids, I had gained about 40 pounds of fluid. These steroids were affecting almost every organ in my body. I recall telling the Lord, *"Please, God, don't let my sickness affect my heart or my mind."* God did grant me that request and protected the most vital parts of my being, my heart and mind, from the effects of this dreadful illness.

When my family and friends visited me and saw the horrible physical condition I was in, they looked at me with compassion and said, "How can you stand the pain and torment of this awful sickness that has inflicted your body?" They were right. As Rose Franco, I was weak, frail and helpless. I literally did not feel like myself while I was going through this sickness. I felt like this was happening to someone else. Some people did not understand the full meaning of what I was feeling. The Holy Spirit, the living dominant force within my being, surpassed the limited endurance of my flesh. Also sustaining me were the endless prayers of my faithful relatives and Christian friends throughout the United States.

Still, the doctors did not fully understand what caused my sickness. Each one had his own medical opinion when evaluating my condition. Therefore, the diagnosis would change from day to day. A conference was held where the various doctors were called in to discuss my medical condition.

My right thumb had lost all feeling and it had turned black. It was swollen and lifeless. The doctors suggested that my thumb might have to be amputated. When I heard this, "I looked at that thumb and I prayed, *"Dear Lord God, my body is the temple of the Holy Spirit and if I am to live, the healing of this thumb will be my miracle, in Jesus Name I pray."* Because of what happened to my thumb, some of the doctors thought I had amyloidosis, a disease that causes the veins to thicken, harden, and reduces the blood flow. To try and confirm this theory, they ordered two biopsies to be performed. To do this they cut a portion of skin and tissue from my body. If I tell you how big the knife was, I'm afraid you'll find it hard to believe. When I saw it in the doctor's hand, I was ready to pass out! Then I heard the doctor tell the nurse, "Don't you have a smaller one?"

One biopsy was done on my stomach, and another one on my ankle. We were first told that one tested positive and the other one tested negative. Later we were told that they were both positive. This left a question on my mind; how could this be? I still believed the results of the first test. I know this might sound foolish to you, but in my heart I believed that God could heal me no matter what sickness the doctors said I had.

In between hospital stays, in December 2001, I was at home when my son Robert came to see me from Virginia with two of my grandchildren, Shawn and Krista. Shawn, an associate pastor at the Cornerstone Assembly of God church in Chester, Virginia, seeing the lifeless infected thumb began praying for me and anointed me with oil. He asked God to restore life and bring healing to my thumb. As of that day, I believe God began healing me of that dreadful disease called amyloidosis. A medical nurse who was nursing my thumb witnessed how God was gradually restoring and bringing life into my thumb. Within a few weeks my thumb had new skin, a new nail and the feeling and life restored completely. The nurse called it "The miracle thumb."

Since I had returned to California, between October 17, 2001, and April 30, 2002, I was admitted nine times to four different hospitals and six times to five different nursing homes. The health insurance only allowed a limited number of days for each hospital stay. This went on for months. They would discharge me, send me home. After being home a few days, the visiting nurses seeing my deteriorating medical condition would call an ambulance and send me back to the hospital. This happened four or five times. I was like a bouncing ball, going back and forth to different hospitals, home and nursing homes.

It seemed that each day the doctors would suggest another test, more medication or another medical term for my illness. Instead of my physical condition improving, it was getting worse by the minute. As I prayed, I knew something was wrong. It was obvious that the effect of these medications was destroying my physical body. Several times I thought to myself, "If God wants me to live, and I stop taking these medications that are killing me, then He will not let me die. But how am I going to get rid of these pills?" There was no possible way for me to do that. The nurses stayed in my room until every pill went down my throat.

My family was still going along with the doctors, thinking that they were nursing me back to health, when all the while these pills were taking my life away. At times I felt that I was alone. It was during these lonely times that I would put all my confidence in God; for He knew what was happening to me beyond what the doctors were telling my family.

One night after talking with the Lord about how I felt concerning my treatment at this hospital, I had a dream about the doctor in charge of my case. *In the dream, he was coming through an arched doorway of a seminary with his arms full of books. As he was walking away from the building, I heard a voice in my dream say, "He has book knowledge, but no wisdom how to use it."*

To confirm my dream, I asked the doctor the next morning, "Where did you receive your medical education?" He told me he went to a seminary school. I asked him to describe the building. Sure enough it was exactly the building I had seen in my dream. *What more did I need to confirm that something was wrong?* I knew that if I were to live, the Lord would have to get me out of this hospital. I thank God for allowing my children to catch the vision of what was going on. They began to seek outside information about the medical treatment my doctors were giving me and research other alternatives.

In the meanwhile, other deplorable and frightening situations had occurred. Let me just mention a few of the less painful ones. Due to the steroids, the skin on my body started to change. It became dry, brittle and rough looking. Gradually the skin on my legs, arms and chest were peeling off. I was aware of how horrible my skin looked. When anyone came to visit me I would tuck my arms under the sheets. It took months for this condition to clear up completely.

Another situation occurred at three o'clock in the morning while I was in a deep sleep. My bed began to shake. I awoke in a state of horror. At first I thought, "What is it, an earthquake?" But as I opened my eyes, I saw nurses and orderlies around my bed. They were moving me to another room. I was so frightened. My body was trembling with fear. "Where are you taking me?"

"To an isolated room," answered the nurse.

"Who gave you permission to move me?" I asked. They all looked at me and didn't say a word. Again I repeated, "I need to know why you are sending me to an isolated room? Please let me call my son. He needs to know what is happening." I called my son and within minutes he was at the hospital.

When my son entered my room he was given protective clothing to wear. He comforted me and then went out to the nurses' station. He asked the nurses, "Why was it so necessary for you to move my mother in the middle of the night while she was in a sound sleep? Didn't you realize how frightening it would be for her? Couldn't you have waited until the morning? And why did she need to be isolated?"

They timidly said, "We're sorry. We were given orders to move her quickly away from the other patients because she has tuberculosis."

"Tuberculosis?" That was all my son had to hear. "I want to know who gave you orders to move her?" My son continued, "I want to see the lab test and the doctor's report."

As soon as my son saw the doctor, he said to him, "After all my mother has been through, now you're telling us she has tuberculosis? How could this happen?" He requested an investigation to verify their findings. They kept me in isolation for several more days. Everyone was so fearful of visiting me because they thought I had this contagious disease.

The result of the investigation was that I did not have tuberculosis. What a sigh of relief was experienced by all of us. I was taken out of the isolation room and sent back to my room. My family had plenty of questions for the doctor and nurses. They were told that the lab or some hospital personnel had made a mistake.

This mistake caused us needless worry, fear and anxiety. We realized that people are human and make mistakes, but when so many are made, you begin to question and you want answers. This is why we must pray whenever anyone goes for tests or goes into the hospital. Be encouraged to know that when the arm of flesh fails us, God will be there to protect and deliver us if our trust is in Him.

During one of my hospital stays, my family was told that my oxygen level was very low and that I had too much carbon dioxide in my body and if it wasn't removed I could die. The doctors' solution was a very serious and dangerous procedure to remove the carbon dioxide. There was still the possibility that I might not pull through. Before I knew it, I found myself enclosed in a tent, with a mask over my face and hooked up to several different machines. I cannot put into words how painful and agonizing it was. I begged for help, telling the technicians, "Please stop, I can't breathe, I'm dying!" Literally, I was dying, but God intervened and kept me alive. After the procedure, I had lost most of the feeling in my hands and feet. I was told by a physical therapist that it was possible that I might not be able to walk because of the numbness. After a few months while watching a TV program, the preacher had a Word of Knowledge that I knew was for me because it described the numbness in my feet. I believed God for my healing and that night the feeling in my feet began to return.

Let me share another incident that occurred at a different hospital. Prior to being admitted to this hospital, I was given a strong medication for a very bad case of sinus infection. The infection was spreading. My daughter was with me when a doctor came into my room. The doctor said, "We are going to do a test on your mother. I will be inserting a tube up her nose. It won't hurt if she cooperates."

The tube was almost as wide as my ring finger. Wow, when I saw how big the tube was, I must admit, I was terribly frightened. I asked the doctor, "Why do you have to do this test?" He didn't answer my question directly. He just told us it was an experimental test. Hearing this, I was overwhelmed with fear and concern.

I tried to refuse the test, but they insisted that I should have it done. Against my better judgment I finally consented. Again, I called on the only one who could help me, none other than my Lord and Savior.

The doctor inserted the tube up my nose about two inches or so. As he did this, blood came gushing out and squirted all over the bed. The doctor became alarmed and discontinued the test. Something happened through this procedure that caused me to lose all of my hearing.

I became totally deaf and I found myself saying, *"Oh, dear Lord, what next? Is there no end to all these awful things that are happening to me one after another? How much more can I take? Lord, please break the power of darkness that is out to destroy my life. Help me and deliver me from this curse of sickness and painful experiences."*

After this prayer I was still deaf, but the Holy Spirit was saying, *"Just keep holding on. I am with you. Just don't give up. Hold on."* Then I heard myself say, *"Lord, if you give me back my hearing, it will be another sign that you are going to heal me completely."* Thank God within about eight days my hearing came back completely.

During my hospital stay prayer requests were called into several Christian television stations. One of my sisters called the Day Star Christian TV Station. She told the counselor that I was critically ill. As they prayed together the counselor had a Word of Knowledge from the Lord, *"The enemy of her soul has brought this sickness upon her body to destroy her, but I will deliver her and heal her. She will go forth in the power of my Spirit and will testify of me and bring my healing message to others."* What an encouraging and uplifting Word from the Lord! It rekindled the fire of hope and life once again.

Not only can Satan bring an illness upon us, but he can also use people to carry out his work. The following are a few of the incidents that happened while I was in the hospital that will witness to the Word of Knowledge that was given by the Holy Spirit.

There was a nurse who I believe was hoping that I would die. At times I couldn't help but wonder how and why I had been placed in her care. My water intake was restricted, but I was allowed a certain number of ounces per day. I begged for a little water, but she wouldn't give me it to me. She insisted that the orders were that I have no water intake, and she even went as far as removing my water pitcher.

I was on a heavy dosage of Lasix medication to eliminate the fluids from my body. I had retained about 40 extra pounds of fluid due to the steroids. I was so dry and thirsty that my tongue was literally going back into my throat. I asked her again, "Please, I'm choking. I need some water!" She looked at me with no compassion and without any remorse and walked away. I can't put in words how desperate I was. I felt my body closing down.

I began to cry. I could barely speak. "Why is she doing this to me? I think she wants me to die." I asked if I could call my husband and she would not let me call him. When my doctor heard what had happened, he said, "You make sure this doesn't happen again. She is to have water, even when it is restricted."

I felt relief when this nurse didn't return to my room for several days. I was hoping and praying that as a visiting nurse, maybe her time was up and she had left the hospital. But sure enough to my disappointment, after a few days, she was back in my room. I looked toward heaven and said, *"Oh, Lord not again!"* There she was pacing the floor in my room as though she had something on her mind. Then she stopped in front of my bed, came close to me, and in a very low voice said, *"Why do you want to live, Rose? You will never be well again and you will be in and out of hospitals. You are making it hard on your family."*

With the little strength I had, I called on the Blood of Jesus to protect me from her. I felt a bad spirit coming from her to discourage me. Right after this happened, my brother came to visit me. I related this incident to him. He reprimanded the nurse for mistreating me and told her, "If this happens again, I will report you to the hospital staff." I believe it was the hundreds of prayers that kept me alive in spite of all this. It was a constant spiritual, mental and physical battle.

Unbeknown to me, the physician in charge of my case had said to my son, *"Why are you trying to hold on to your mother? Let go of her. You will make it easier on her if you let her go. If she lives, she will never be well and will be in and out of hospitals. She had a good life and a good family, so why not let her go?"*

My son had a good answer for him, *"Doctor, do you have a mother? Would you say that about your mother? Let me tell you doctor, if I were in that bed and my mother was in my place, she would never give up on me."* With this moving statement it's not surprising that the doctor did not have an answer for my son.

My daughter, son, husband and brother came to the hospital almost every day. All they heard from the doctors, with the exception of one doctor, were negative and discouraging reports. Even though with the human eye my dying condition was very obvious, they never lost hope and faith in God for my healing.

Yes, there were times that I would tell my family, "Why doesn't God take me out of this misery and bring me home with Him?"

They would respond by saying, "God must still have a work for you to do." It was hard for me to see them suffer along with me. They spent endless hours researching and communicating with the Mayo Clinic about my medical condition as diagnosed by the doctors on my case. I was more concerned about the effect my sickness was having on my family than it did on me.

They were spending days and nights at the hospitals keeping up with my medical reports and the hospital care. My daughter and my husband took turns staying overnight sleeping on uncomfortable chairs. My son John had black rings under his eyes from lack of sleep. He compiled all my medical records during my illness and organized them in large folders. He would come after work and stay until midnight, go home, get a few hours sleep and leave for work at five a.m. They worked feverishly holding on to every little bit of hope for my recovery.

I was in the hospital during the Christmas holidays. I will never forget my son John coming into my room with the most beautiful three-foot artificial tree on Christmas Eve. Instead of going home to be with his family and in-laws, he patiently hung every ornament and decoration with so much care and love. The Christmas tree became the center of attention. Everyone who entered my room admired this symbol of love. My son did not stop there. He bought gifts for each doctor and for the nurses.

Among all of the eight doctors, there was one who did not make light of my faith in God. After we discussed my medical condition, I told him, "God has healed me in the past and I know He can heal me now."

Then as the doctor was leaving my room he turned to my son and said, "Your mother has a good thing going for her."

When the other doctors were implying there was no hope for my recovery, I would tell them, "I know that if God wants me to live,

I will live. If he created my body, then what is it for Him to heal me? He is my Great Physician." I could tell that my doctor did not agree with what I was saying, but that did not weaken my strong faith in God. He told my family that I was losing it, suggesting that my illness was affecting my mind. He went on to say, "We can give her medication for her mental condition."

With this, my family was concerned as to what the doctors might do to me. Reluctantly they told me not to express my thoughts to the doctors. "They think something is wrong with you when you speak about your faith in God." I told my family, *"I will not take any tranquilizers or mood-changing medication. I have every right to express my faith in God. He is the only one sustaining me and keeping me through all of this suffering."* If I had listened to what the doctors were saying about my faith in God, I would not be alive today to share my miracle.

After being discharged from the hospital, as usual I was sent to a nursing home. While I was lying in bed, I was thinking about what the doctor had said about my faith in God. I began sharing my heartache with the Lord, *"Please, God, the only thing I have to help me is my faith in you. You are my anchor, my life, and my strength. Now they are attacking my faith in you, saying that I am losing my mind. I'm tired, weary and worn. I cannot hold on any longer. You know I love you, Lord. Please hear my prayer."* I kept crying out to God uncontrollably. The woman in the bed next to me tried to console me, but I experienced no relief.

It was around ten in the evening and no visitors were allowed in our room at that hour besides my family. But that evening a man came into my room while I was crying and talking to the Lord. He came close to my bed and said, *"Your sufferings are to bring healing to others."*

As he said that, I said to myself, "Lord, why do I have to suffer to bring healing to others?"

I did not say a word; yet he spoke again saying, *"Remember the suffering of Jesus."* He patted me on the shoulder and left the room.

My roommate witnessed what had just taken place. This man had to be an angel in disguise sent by God to comfort me. After this angelic encounter all I could say was, *"Lord how can I complain when you suffered so much for me and for the salvation of humanity. Please forgive me. And if you want to use my sickness to bring healing to others then Lord help me to trust you for my healing."*

Between the pain and suffering, at times I was only holding on to the Lord with one little finger, but I did not let go. Many times I would sing, *"Precious Lord, take my hand, lead me on, let me stand. I am tired, I am weak, I am worn. Through the storm, through the night, lead me on to the light. Precious Lord, take my hand, lead me on."*

I recall that weeks later, back in the hospital, while my daughter and son were in my room, I was told that I was going to have a special lung test performed on me in the morning. After the visitation of that angel in disguise, I had regained a sense of new hope, but hearing those words again ANOTHER TEST, it just blew my mind! I asked the Lord, *"When is this going to end, Lord? I thought the tests were over. What are they looking for now?"* Only my family and a few loved ones who had visited me and witnessed these unbelievable happenings could understand the intensity of this trial.

I wanted my daughter to stay with me that night, but she was scheduled to leave for New York the next morning. The nurse, knowing this, told her to leave and said, "You don't have to worry; I'll look after her." My children did not want to leave me in this condition. But again the nurse insisted that they should leave. Only God knew how badly I needed them to stay with me that night. Satan wasted no time in telling me, "They don't love you or care about you; otherwise, they would not leave you in this condition."

I wondered why they were listening to the nurse when I told them to please stay with me a little longer. Again, Satan was trying to break my spirit and infiltrate my mind with self-pity. He is a liar and a deceiver of men. He has a unique way of distorting the truth. In my weakness, I knew that my children loved me and were doing everything within their power for my recovery. I had asked God to forgive me for holding it against my dear children.

The nurse had closed my door right after my children left and never returned to my room. The only woman who entered my room while I was crying was a respiratory technician. I was having difficulty breathing. She tried to comfort me and stayed with me for a few minutes and said, "You shouldn't be alone. I'll try to come back when I finish my rounds." She meant well, but she never came back. In fact, no one came into my room to check on me as they had promised my children.

For two straight hours after my children left, I cried and cried until I was too weak to cry anymore. I felt discouraged, and let down. I finally gave my thoughts over to the only one who could comfort me, my Lord and Savior. I actually begged the Lord from the innermost part of my being, "Oh my Lord, if you love me please take me home with you. Lord, don't let me suffer any longer, just let me die peacefully." After calling out to God, a remarkable and unexplainable peace came over me. My room was filled with the divine presence of God. All my sorrow seemed to be lifted. I first started to speak in my heavenly language to the Lord, a language that only the Lord and my spirit understood.

My spirit was nourished and strengthened. I began singing audibly the words of all these precious uplifting songs: *"Shut in with God in a secret place, there in His presence beholding His face, finding more power to run in the race, I long to be shut in with God."* *"Come by here, dear Lord. Come by here. Somebody needs you. Lord, come by here. Oh Lord, come by here."* One song after another kept coming from the innermost part of my being. *"Come, Holy Spirit, I need you. Come, sweet Spirit, I pray. Come in thy strength and thy power. Come in thy own special way."* *"Spirit of God, I'm empty without you. Spirit of God, come now and fill me. Spirit of God, please flow through me. Holy anointing, fresh Spirit of God, how I need thee."* I was the only patient in the room at that time, and I just kept singing loudly until three in the morning when I fell asleep.

Even though the nurse never came back to my room that night, I did have one special visitor come to my room. It was the third person of the trinity, the Comforter, none other then the Holy Spirit of the Living God.

The next morning, the doctor who was scheduled to perform this very serious lung test came into my room. After God's intervention the night before, all my anxiety and fear was gone. I had no concern about the test. I just had a wonderful peace. The doctor greeted me and gave me a little examination. Then he turned to the nurse and said, "I cannot perform this test on her. She is too weak."

Maybe I would not have survived the test. The Lord already knew that and intervened and again probably spared my life. Thank God, I never did have that test after all.

How can I not recall the time when my brother visited me at the hospital! The doctors told him I had Leukemia and that there was no hope for my recovery. He offered a prayer to God for my healing, one I will never forget. He prayed audibly and was not concerned whether anyone would hear him. He was desperate for God to deliver me from this bed of affliction. *"In the Name of Jesus I rebuke the forces of evil and of sickness and command you to leave in the Name of Jesus. My sister is a child of God and you have no power over her. Get your hands off of her. She will live and be well and she will testify of the healing power of the Lord Jesus."* This was true faith in action and I believe the Lord heard his prayer. My Spirit was lifted and my faith renewed.

A few days later, my family told me that the doctors had ordered a bone marrow test. I had gone through so much that I was reluctant and also afraid of the test. But I realized it would show if I had leukemia or whether I was healed. The night before I had the test,

I called on my great physician, *"Lord Jesus, you know I have a fear about this test, but if you want me to have this test done, please give me a peace about it."*

Then I heard the Lord say, *"Pray before you have the test done."* I started to rehearse a prayer, thinking that I would say the prayer.

The next morning while my family, brother and his wife were visiting me, a doctor whom I did not know came in the room with his assistant. He introduced himself and said, "I will be performing the bone marrow test." I did not hold back. I immediately said to the him, "Doctor, I don't know if you believe in prayer, but I was praying last night and I feel we should pray before doing the procedure." Without any hesitation he said, "Yes, let's pray." I had my mouth open ready to pray and guess what? To my surprise, the doctor grabbed my hand, the others all held hands, and he began to pray.

What a wonderful prayer went up to the throne of God. He told me I would experience pain during the procedure and afterwards, but I did not experience any pain at all. After the test was completed, the doctor told us that he was not the scheduled doctor to perform the test. He said he just happened to be in the hospital, and he was asked to do the bone marrow test. I believe God had it all planned for the faith-believing doctor to do this procedure instead of the doctor who was originally scheduled.

A few days later, an oncologist came into my room, sat in a chair and gave me the good news. The results of the bone marrow test showed that the configuration of the biological specimens was not what they were looking for. I looked at the doctor with a sigh of relief, and all I could say was, "Thank God!" But even with this report, the doctors were still treating me for the same sickness. The steroids were draining every bit of strength that I had. I needed help to stand, or even turn side to side in my bed. Unbeknown to me, the doctors told my family that I had only two weeks to live.

My children told the doctors that they were dissatisfied with the medical care I was getting at this hospital. They felt that there must be something more that could be done to save my life. They had been communicating with a top physician at Mayo Clinic and sharing my treatment with him. He wanted me to go to his clinic. Due to the seriousness of my sickness, he suggested that I go to a doctor at UCLA who was recommended to my son because he was highly recognized in the field of Oncology.

The doctors at the hospital where I was did not want me to go to UCLA. They told my family, "Do you think they can do more for her than what we are doing here?" They were giving us a hard time. In spite of all this the children wasted no time. My children made contact with the doctor at UCLA, and within two days I was in his office. He took one look at me lying on a stretcher and told my family, "She is gone. But get her away from the eight doctors and we'll get her off the steroids and I'll admit her to our hospital."

I was a patient at UCLA for 15 days. First with God's help, excellent medical care and good healthy meals my health began to improve. The doctors started the process of getting me off steroids. I believe God gave me this doctor, another angel in disguise. He did not allow the negative diagnoses from the previous doctors to interfere with the faith he had for my recovery. I told the doctor that his hands were in the hands of God and as they worked together, I would recover from this sickness. He smiled and nodded his head in agreement. This was the beginning of my journey back to good health.

From there I was sent to a rehab nursing home for physical therapy, which helped me to gradually regain my strength.

After being discharged from the rehab nursing home, I finally returned to my home. We left the health insurance group that I had before UCLA and went with another subsidiary plan. My family prayed about my future health care. Proverbs 3:6 states, "In all of thy ways acknowledge him, and he shall direct thy paths." When we put God first, He will direct us to make the right decision. My children did their homework and found a good health plan. It was associated with one of the best known hospitals in California.

My new doctors followed the care recommended by the UCLA doctor. They all treated me as a person who would live and not die especially my new oncologist. I was gradually taken off of the 40 medications, including the steroids. The diabetes left and my blood pressure went down to normal. I had the opportunity to witness to the doctors of the healing power of our Lord Jesus.

Thank God, within months I was back to good health, going with my husband to his evangelistic meetings and giving my healing testimony. Praise the Lord.

Recently I went to visit the UCLA doctor. I brought him a business card holder with scriptures especially made for physicians. When he saw me, he said, "I'm sorry, should I know you?" I reminded him of the day I entered his office on a stretcher. He said, "I would have never known that it was you, Rose. Oh my, you look wonderful." I gave him a plaque expressing my thanks to him for assisting God in my recovery that extended my life. We said a prayer with him and left. We did the same for two other doctors who took care of me after I left UCLA. They all knew my healing was a miracle.

There was only one doctor from the previous hospital who had said, "Your mother has a good thing going for her." This remark left an impression on my heart. I felt that I had to thank him as well. We stopped by his office to give him a similar gift and plaque. He came into the waiting room, looked at me and said, "Rose, I would have never recognized you. But your husband yes, but you, no, never."

We spoke to him about the miracle that God had performed in my life. We asked, "Doctor, do you have a Bible?"

He replied, "Yes, my devout Christian son recently gave me one." I quoted a few scriptures to him, and then he said, "I did not know that was in the Bible."

He was so elated over what God did for me that he just stayed on talking with us until his nurse called him, even though there were patients waiting for him.

I would like to share the letter that we received from this doctor. *"It was very nice to see you and to know that Rose is well now. I was very touched by your framed letter of appreciation and the lovely little plaque of the 'Doctor's Prayer.' I have them displayed in my private office. I will remember you when I look at them. I wish you and your family good health and good future. God bless."*

When we go the extra mile and show God's love through a word, a gift of appreciation or just a smile, it will go a long way in blessing someone's life. Lord, help us to shed your love and living word to those we come in contact with on our earthly journey.

Before concluding my healing testimony, I want to give praise to the doctors God brought into my life who believed in my recovery, to those who prayed for me, and to the good nurses and aides who were diligent on my behalf, caring and helping me during this time.

"Your suffering is to bring healing to others." This word has already come to fulfillment. Also, the words that God gave to the Day Star TV counselor at the beginning of my sickness came to pass. *"The enemy of her soul has brought this sickness upon her body to destroy her, but I will deliver her and heal her. She will go forth in the power of my Spirit and will testify of me and bring my healing message to others, saith the Lord."*

When doctors gave me only two weeks to live, and plans were made for my funeral, my Lord who was with me through it all delivered me from death and extended my life to be a living testimony of his saving and healing power.

I pray that this testimony will be a motivating faith-builder bringing healing to His people, in body, mind and spirit.

Chapter Two

INCREDIBLE MULTIPLE MIRACLES

The Pancake House Miracle

On my way home after teaching morning art classes at the elementary school, I stopped at John's Pancake House for a quick lunch. I had mixed feelings about stopping for lunch, knowing I had to be home at a certain time. But, another voice within me said, "Why don't you stop and relax for a while before going home."

I thought, "Well, it would do me good to have a little time of quietness and relaxation before facing all I have to do at home."

April, the cashier at the restaurant, attended our church in Buffalo. When April saw me entering the restaurant, she was so excited. She immediately turned to me and said, "Mrs. Franco, am I glad to see you!"

I ushered myself to a table in the far corner where I could enjoy some peace and quiet, but this was not to be. Within minutes, April came to the table where I was sitting. Excitedly she said, "Mrs. Franco, you can never know how happy I was when I saw you come into the restaurant. The timing is perfect. Tina, one of my friends came into the restaurant just before you arrived. She is sitting at the table farthest away from you. Tina is going to the hospital tomorrow for surgery because she has a large malignant tumor the size of a grapefruit in her uterus. She has taken a three-month leave of absence from her job for her recovery period. She is extremely worried about her surgery. Would you please go to her table and pray for her?"

I told April, "I would be happy to pray for her." Physically and mentally I felt exhausted after teaching art classes all morning. I realized that my plans for relaxing and unwinding were not going to happen. Then I heard the small still voice of the Holy Spirit saying, *"It is not by chance that you find yourself here. I brought you here at this time for a reason."*

As April and I were on our way to join her friend Tina, I silently prayed, *"Lord if you want to do something here today, please strengthen my mind and body for whatever the Holy Spirit wants to do. Go before us I pray."* After this quick prayer, I felt relaxed and refreshed. It seemed that all my tiredness had disappeared. It is amazing what God can do when we fully depend on Him!

When we reached the table where Tina was sitting, April graciously introduced me to her. They both sat on the opposite side of the table facing me. Tina, with tears in her eyes, began telling me about her medical condition.

I listened to her for awhile. Then I felt the Holy Spirit compelling me to talk to her about the most important decision each one of us must face in life. I told her, "Tina, I must ask you the question that confronts each one of us. If God were to call you home today, to your eternal destination, would you be ready to meet Him?"

She looked at me in amazement, as if to say what do you mean? I began sharing the plan of salvation with her. "Tina, Jesus died on the cross for our sins. That was the price He paid to give us eternal life. Through the sufferings He bore on the cross, healing for our sickness was made possible. The Bible says in John 3:16, 'For God so loved the world, that he gave his only begotten Son, that whosoever believeth in Him should not perish, but have everlasting life.' All you have to do is believe that Jesus is the Son of God, ask Him to forgive your sins, and invite Him into your heart as your Lord and Savior. Tina, the choice is yours. Jesus loves you. He wants to give you peace and joy, and to free you from the bondage of sin."

Tina absorbed every word that I spoke as though she had never heard them before. I believe the Holy Spirit was dealing with her heart. She was ready to receive Christ. With tears flowing down her cheeks she said, "I want Jesus to come into my life. What must I do?" Then she repeated the Sinner's Prayer with me. As she accepted Christ into her life, her face was glowing with the presence of God. Praise the Lord! Little did we know that this was just the beginning of what God was going to do for Tina.

April, the cashier, knew about the miracles God had performed in my life and asked me to share one of them with Tina. I began sharing my testimony about the near fatal accident and the two healing miracles that followed. I told her, "The same healing virtue that invaded my body is available for you. All you have to do is believe in your heart that all things are possible with God."

Tina began weeping uncontrollably and said, "I do believe that God can heal me." We joined our hearts as one and put our hands together across the table. I quoted what Jesus said in Matthew 18:19-20. "Again I say unto you, That if two of you shall agree on earth as touching any thing that they shall ask, it shall be done for them of my

Father which is in heaven. For where two or three are gathered together in my name, there am I in the midst of them."

Now that the three of us were in agreement with the Word of God, I offered up a simple prayer to the throne of God. *"Our Father we come before thee in the name of Jesus Christ, your son, and in the power of the Holy Spirit. We thank you Lord for Tina and her commitment to you. Now as we have joined our hearts together as one with you, we come in faith believing for the healing of Tina's body. We come against this tumor in the Name of Jesus. We command it to be uprooted and to dry up and shrink. In Jesus' Name we ask it, Amen!"*

Before leaving the restaurant I said, "Tina, we will be praying for you. Remember you are not alone, the Lord is with you. We will visit you at the hospital. Here is my phone number if you need to call me. "

On my way home I was rejoicing and thanking the Lord for Tina's salvation. I was so blessed that as I drove I began speaking in my heavenly language. As I approached a red light, a man in the car to the right of me was staring at me, thinking it strange that I was talking to myself. Little did he know that I was not alone in the car, but that the Lord was with me, and I was communicating with Him through the Holy Spirit.

About an hour after I arrived at home, my phone rang. It was Tina. As I picked up the phone, I heard, "Oh, Mrs. Franco, I'm so excited. I can barely talk."

I asked Tina, "What is it? Are you all right?"

"Yes, I think so, but I don't know what happened. I just made it home in time before all this fluid came gushing out of my body. What shall I do?"

"Tina, call your doctor and tell him exactly what happened."

When Tina's doctor heard this, he said, "Good, I want you to keep the appointment at the hospital for tomorrow morning. I will perform a D and C procedure instead of surgery and see what happened. I will see you at the hospital."

The next day at the hospital the doctor had an unbelievable surprise when he performed the D and C procedure. He told Tina, "I don't understand what happened here! The only thing I found in the uterus was a dried up outer shell of the tumor. And the good news is that the cancer is all gone." This is what every cancer stricken patient wants to hear!

Again the doctor repeated, "No more cancer! It's not normal for this to happen. This has to be a miracle!"

Tina knew what had happened. Her new faith in God, the healer of sickness, brought about this miracle.

That evening Mrs. Moore and I visited Tina at the hospital. When we heard the good news, we couldn't help but praise God for the miracle. While we were there, Tina began experiencing some normal pain that is associated with having a D and C. Once again, the Lord proved Himself to Tina that He is the Great Physician and Healer. As we prayed for her, she said, "The pain is gone! It's hard to believe, but truly all my pain is gone. Thank God."

Here is a woman who had taken a three-month leave of absence from her job for the anticipated length of time needed for her recovery. But God had a different plan for her life. Because of her faith in the Lord she received total healing and was discharged from the hospital the next day. And better yet, on Sunday morning she was at our church thanking God for her double miracle, the salvation of her soul and the healing of her body. You can imagine how the body of Christ was rejoicing!

I know you agree with me that God is everywhere and anywhere at any given time. I want you to think about where this miracle took place. It wasn't in church. It wasn't at a massive healing meeting. It was at a Pancake House surrounded with customers; yet God was still there. I believe this miracle was the product of believing the Word of God, exercising faith in the Word and agreeing as one for the healing. Man cannot heal. They can only assist the healing hand of God.

This is what God can do if you can believe and stand firm on His promises. I encourage you to put aside your limited thinking and claim your healing. He made the provision for you to receive healing for body, mind and spirit through His perfect sacrifice on Mount Calvary.

This same Jesus who visited Tina in a Pancake House and gave her a twofold miracle loves you and cares about your need. Ask in faith believing for your answer to come in His way and in His timing.

A Doctor's Miracle

It happened in the spring of 1992 while I was working part-time at a real estate company. I had listed a motel property in the

Hampton Bays, an hour away from our home. My husband and I drove an interested client to see the property. On the way back I dropped my husband off at our home. Then I went to the office, just four minutes away, to check my messages.

On the way to the office, I stopped for a red light at an intersection. As I waited for the light to change, a car suddenly hit the back of my car.

Due to the impact of the collision, I suffered several injuries. I went to a chiropractor for treatment, hoping to receive some relief from the pain I was experiencing. The doctor was about to take some x-rays of my injuries when he stopped and began asking me about my medical history. I told him about a healing miracle I had experienced. "Doctor, 19 years ago, God healed me of injuries I sustained in another car accident, so what is it for Him to heal me of these injuries?"

After sharing this miraculous testimony with the doctor, he gave me a treatment but no x-rays. Instead he sent me to see a neurologist for further tests.

The neurologist ordered several tests. Then he gave me medication for pain, and said, "Rose, get plenty of rest and continue with your chiropractic treatments."

For the first few weeks I was unable to work. Gradually, I was able to work limited hours from home. Still having much pain, the doctor advised me to limit my driving. I started to work two or three half days per week with the help of an agent.

My insurance company sent me to different doctors to evaluate my medical condition. They scheduled me for an appointment to see a doctor in New York about the same time as we were holding meetings in Florida. I told them I was unable to keep that appointment, and their response was, "No problem, Rose, we'll schedule an appointment for you with a chiropractor in Florida."

Within a few days, I received a letter with the date and time of my appointment with a Dr. Jeff in Florida. I became upset and I told my husband, "John, why doesn't the Lord heal me? I am sick and tired of going to all these different doctors." He just listened patiently and said nothing. Then I asked my husband, "Will you drive me to this doctor's office?"

Without hesitation he said, "Rose, just relax. I'll come with you."

I went back to the kitchen to do some cleaning. As I was washing dishes, still upset and discouraged, I heard the Holy Spirit whisper in my thoughts saying, "Why are you fretting? Fret not!" Immediately a peace came over me and all the anxiety left!

The day of my appointment arrived. We were given directions to the doctor's office. With a little guidance from a local street map we had no problem finding the office. I had my MRI report with me. My turn came to see Dr. Jeff. He gave me a complete checkup. He was disappointed because the insurance company had refused his request to take x-rays of my back. He couldn't understand why my chiropractor back in New York had not taken x-rays.

I told him, "Doctor, I have my MRI report with me that you can read." But he still preferred seeing an x-ray.

At this point in our conversation I could hear in my spirit, "Tell him what happened and the reason why your doctor did not take the x-rays. Don't hold back!"

After hearing this, I said, "Doctor, are you through with my examination?"

He answered, "Yes, Rose."

"Let me tell you exactly what happened." I told Dr. Jeff what I had told my chiropractor back in New York, how God had completely healed me of such grave injuries in the past. I said, "If God did it then, what is it for Him to heal me now?" For whatever reason, my doctor in New York did not take any x-rays.

Dr. Jeff became interested and was curious to know more about my healing miracle.

He asked me, "Rose, what is your religious belief?" I told him that I believe in salvation through Jesus Christ and I quoted John 3:16. I went on to tell him that I believe in receiving the infilling of the Holy Spirit, and I quoted scripture from John chapter 14 and Acts 2:4.

As I shared my belief according to the Word of God, with excitement he spoke up and said, "This is what I want. When I was in medical school, a fellow student invited me to her church. They believed in receiving the Holy Spirit experience! I want to come to your church."

"My husband no longer pastors a church. He has been ministering as an evangelist and speaks at different churches."

"Rose, I want to come to one of his services."

After my examination, we both went back to the waiting room. I introduced him to my husband. A friendship and a bond of God's love were drawing us together as we shared the things of God.

While all this was going on, unexpectedly Dr. Jeff's mother walked into the waiting room. The doctor looked surprised, but at the same time he was happy to see her. He introduced us to her. He shared with her the experience he had had at medical school with a fellow student, and explained to her that we were of the same religious belief as his fellow student.

After concluding our conversation, Dr. Jeff and his mother anxiously said, "Please give us the address of the Miami church where you will be speaking this coming Sunday. We want to come to your meeting."

Dr. Jeff came alone to the service that day. The service was already in progress when the doctor arrived. He came into the church and sat between the pastor's wife and me. We were standing and singing choruses. The doctor immediately joined us in singing. Then he turned to me and said, "Rose, you brought me to the right place."

He was moved by the presence of the Lord that was evident in the service. During an altar call he went up for prayer and renewed his relationship with the Lord. The touch of God was upon his life. He was experiencing an overwhelming joy that brought tears to his eyes.

This was only the beginning of what God was about to do in Dr. Jeff's life. His love for God and the Word was met with opposition from his coworkers. The office where Dr. Jeff was working when we first met, had dismissed him from their practice. Anyone who had the privilege of knowing Dr. Jeff spoke very highly of him as a doctor and as a person. Why would anyone want to dismiss a good doctor like Dr. Jeff? One might find the complaint they had against the doctor hard to believe. They told him the reason why they dismissed him was because *he mentioned his God once too many times.*

This was Dr. Jeff's first spiritual trial after he had renewed his relationship with Christ. However, what was meant for bad, God turned around for good. God had something in store for Dr. Jeff, much better than that situation. God honored and exalted him with greater blessings both materially and spiritually. But along the way he was to experience an even greater trial.

We kept in touch with Dr. Jeff by telephone. Several times while we were ministering in Florida, the doctor would attend our services. We prayed with him that God would use him for His honor and glory.

While all this was happening suddenly he became critically ill. He lost a lot of weight and strength in his body due to the sickness. It was heartbreaking for us to hear this dreadful news. We had grown to love him not only as a brother in Christ, but as a son. We just could not give up on his healing. God had a ministry for this loving, caring, handsome young doctor.

We had every church, in different parts of the country wherever we ministered, praying for Dr. Jeff's healing. When we returned to Florida for services, we made a call to Dr. Jeff. He came with his mother to our service that was held at the Upper Room Assembly of God Church in South Miami.

It was the first time we had seen the doctor in person since this dreadful illness had invaded his body. As I greeted him, I could see that he was so thin and sickly. My heart was touched and I grieved with compassion and concern. I cried out to God both inwardly and outwardly, *"Lord, you caused our paths to meet for a purpose beyond this illness. I know he loves You and wants to serve You and Your people. Please, Lord, touch him with your healing virtue and deliver him from this sickness. Make him a living testimony of your healing power. I pray that many souls will come to know you through his life."*

Through the whole service my prayer was being uttered quietly before the Lord. At the end of the service, many souls went up for prayer including Dr. Jeff and his mother. I also went up and joined them at the altar.

As Dr. Jeff was praying, one of the ministers laid hands on him. The anointing of God's power fell upon him. When that happened, I believe God touched Dr. Jeff and the healing process began in his body. Another pastor went to the doctor's mother and asked her to go pray over her son. As she did, she received the baptism in the Holy Spirit. This was all new to her and she did not understand what really happened. She later told her son about the heavenly language she was speaking. Dr. Jeff told his mother that it was the manifestation of the Holy Spirit! What a glorious morning that was!

In June, we returned to New York where we had a full schedule of meetings booked. We continued to request prayer for Dr. Jeff at every service.

During the fall months of that year, I kept having Dr. Jeff before me not only in my prayer, but every time I turned around I would see his face.

After sharing this with my husband, he said, "Why don't you give him a call and let him know we are praying for him." I picked up the phone and dialed the doctor's phone number, but I was unable to reach him. My second thought was to call his mother.

When she heard my voice she was bubbling over with joy. "Mrs. Franco, you were unable to reach my son because he went on a skiing trip in Colorado." She went on to say, "He is almost 100 percent healed. Thank God!" I was rejoicing and thanking God with her for the miracle. What a tremendous testimony of the faithfulness of God!

We went back to Florida in the spring of the following year. Dr. Jeff came with his mother and shared his healing testimony at the church where we were ministering. As he shared the miracle of his healing, the people were blessed, uplifted and encouraged to believe God for their miracle.

This sickness was another trial for Dr. Jeff, but God victoriously brought him through. He is a testimony of God's goodness and healing power.

What has happened with Dr. Jeff's practice? He opened his own office and it is flourishing. It is called, "Lord's Chiropractic and Puantum Medicine Center in Ft. Lauderdale, Florida." Dr. Jeff and other doctors who work for him minister to the needs of the whole person. In his office, you will see scripture verses in every room. He witnesses to his patients and souls are being won to the Lord.

God gave him abundantly more than what was taken away from him. Again, what was meant for evil, God turned around for good because Dr. Jeff dared to put God first in his life.

There were many steps in God's plan that brought about a renewed relationship with Christ, a healing and prosperity. It began with the absence of x-rays, my healing testimony, and sharing my religious beliefs about salvation and the baptism in the Holy Spirit. Dr. Jeff's Christian journey began with him losing his job because of his beliefs, and then having a dreadful sickness that almost destroyed him. But God restored and healed him completely and provided a flourishing medical practice where he now witnesses for the Lord. In addition, God blessed him with a wonderful Christian wife and a beautiful baby girl.

God can use us if we are willing, as instruments to bring about his will and purpose in the lives of others. We are His hands, His feet and His verbal utterance!

We should never hold back when the Holy Spirit gives us a word to share. If so, this would have been just another doctor's visit. Remember that you may be the only vehicle through which someone will come to know the Lord.

Triple Miracles during Hospital Stay

While living in Arizona, I was teaching at a college, so that we could make ends meet. I went to the doctor because I was suffering with severe pains in my stomach. He admitted me into a hospital for diagnostic tests. The results of the tests showed that I had a hiatal hernia. My stay at the hospital was extended for several more days.

At first there was one other patient in my room. She was in the bed to the left of me. I will refer to her as Mary. Mary was the aunt of a famous actress and singer. She was a good Baptist who read her Bible every morning. Mary and I became friends. We prayed together over our meals every day. We had a lot in common about the things of God.

On the third day another patient was brought into our room. She was in the bed to the right of me, putting my bed in the middle of both patients. Her name was Betty. Betty kept to herself. Her curtains were drawn most of the time. In the morning she went down for x-rays. Later in the afternoon her doctor came to visit her, and as soon as he left the room, she began crying. Mary, hearing this said, "Rose, why don't you go and pray for her. I will be here praying with you."

As usual, I prayed before approaching Betty and asked the Lord to go before me. The Holy Spirit gave me the words that were needed in that situation. I went by her bedside and tried to comfort her, but before I could say another word she told me the sad news that the doctor had just given her. He told Betty that she had a malignant tumor on her pituitary gland and she would need surgery.

She needed to hear about the Great Physician, Jesus who could heal her body, soul and spirit. As I shared the Word of God with her and the sacrifice of Jesus, I sensed that she didn't seem to know much about the Lord. I told her that the Lord Jesus was desirous to come into her heart, forgive her sins and give her new life, peace and joy in the midst of her sickness. With tears streaming down her face, she openly accepted the Lord Jesus. I shared with her that Mary and I were believing God for her healing. Betty hearing that Jesus is also a healer said, "Rose, I want to believe with you and Mary for Jesus to heal me. I don't know what to say. This is all new to me. Please pray for me." As we prayed and came against the tumor in the Name of Jesus, we could sense an overwhelming presence of the Holy Spirit. As it is written in Zechariah 4:6b, "Not by might, nor by power, but by my Spirit, saith the Lord of host."

I cannot put into words how Mary and I were rejoicing over another soul that had come to the Lord. This was the first miracle and the most important one that happened through that prayer.

The next morning the doctor told Betty she was going down for another x-ray to show the exact position of the tumor before they would operate on her the following day. Betty's husband and family were to come to the hospital that night to discuss the surgery with the doctor and what could happen with this type of operation.

Evening came and the family gathered together with sad expressions on their faces. Minutes later the doctor arrived, and they partially drew the curtains. Mary was anxious to hear what the doctor had to say. She turned to me and said, "Rose, listen to what the doctor is saying." I was only about two feet away from the partially drawn curtain. I could hear and see what was going on.

The doctor had a diagram of the pituitary gland. He kept explaining about the gland and its function and then he hesitated. Betty's husband became upset and said, "I want to hear about the tumor and the surgery. Show us the tumor."

The Doctor quietly said, "We took x-rays again this morning and we don't know what happened, but the tumor is gone." You can imagine the joy and excitement that filled the room. Mary and I were thanking God for Betty's two fold miracles: salvation and physical healing. Later I encouraged Betty to attend a Bible believing church with her family and to stay faithful to the Lord.

Mary was discharged the next day, and I was discharged two days later. There were three miracles that happened while praying for Betty. I was not aware of the third miracle until three months later, when we moved back to Long Island.

Anyone who has experienced moving a number of times knows that it isn't an easy task. We left Arizona and traveled to New York overnight. Going without sleep was no picnic. When we arrived at the Long Island residence, and seeing the condition it was in, my husband and I were devastated. Tired as we were, we began cleaning the house and washing floors the same day we arrived. Later that evening my son invited us to his home for dinner. As I was eating, I suddenly became weak and I excused myself. As I headed for the bathroom I began feeling faint and dizzy. I called out to my husband and my son as I started to pass out.

My son called his neighbor who is a pharmacist. He was unable to feel my pulse and said, "Get her to the hospital right away!" When we arrived there, the doctor asked about my medical history. I told him I had been in a hospital several months earlier with a hiatal hernia. The doctor ordered x-rays the next day.

He came to my room that afternoon and showed us the x-rays. He looked at me and my husband and said, "Mrs. Franco, did you say you have a hiatal hernia?"

My husband answered, "Yes Doctor, I saw it on the x-rays that were taken in Arizona. The hiatal hernia was very visible and obvious. In fact the doctor at that hospital mentioned surgery, and he said, 'This type of surgery is not always successful. It is better to wait.'"

The doctor looked at us and said, "Well, I don't know what happened, and I certainly can't explain it, but she doesn't have the hiatal hernia now!"

My husband looked at me and then at the doctor and said, "Doctor it's got to be a miracle, thank God."

The doctor answered, "I agree!"

Then the Holy Spirit spoke to me saying, *"While you put aside your own sickness and were ministering to the needs of others, I was healing your body."* Then it all came back to me like a flash.

That word from the Holy Spirit was so true. When we care for others and take our mind off of ourselves, the Lord takes care to our needs whatever they may be. I believe God purposed for me to be admitted to the Long Island Hospital where x-rays were taken again to verify my healing that had taken place in Arizona. To God be the glory, great things He has done! Not only one miracle, or two miracles, but also three miracles took place in a hospital setting where patients go and are treated by medical doctors. On that special day the great physician, Doctor Jesus, was called in and performed three miracles.

Chapter Three

MIRACLES OF PROVISION

The Last Ten Dollars

Before going into full-time ministry, my husband and I were both working making a comfortable living. We owned some commercial lots located along side a highway. When we took on our first pastorate, our salary went down to about 75 dollars per week, about one-third of what we were making previously. With the living expenses needed to raise three children, we found it to be a financial challenge. We had to sell the commercial lots to meet our obligations. We were living from week to week.

There were several needy families in the church. In one particular situation the husband, breadwinner of the family, was incapacitated due to a work-related injury. They had five children, all young in age. The first time we visited them at their home, we could hardly sit on their chairs. The springs on the cushions were protruding. We took their chairs home with us, repaired and recovered them. The electricity and gas were shut off for lack of money. My husband paid their bills.

The wife was expecting another child and had no hospitalization. I knew there was no way that we could help them with such a big expense, but I felt a burden for their need. As I prayed about it, I heard the Holy Spirit say, *"Write to the physician, the hospital and some of the churches in the area and share the need."* I was a little shy about doing it, but an inner courage sprang up within me, *"You can do it. You are doing it for Me."* I obeyed the Lord and sent out the letters. The doors of mercy were opened. Each recipient willingly responded to the need presented in the letter. The bills for the doctors, delivery and hospital were all dropped. Our church gave a baby shower, one of the other churches gave money and another one gave food supplies. *When God gives us a burden for the needs of others and we act upon it, He makes the need become a reality through us or by other means.*

It was the end of August when we heard that the two young girls in this family could not start school because they did not have decent clothes to wear. That week, we only had ten dollars left to our name. Before the ministry, like everyone else, I would shop and buy my children new clothes for school. As I thought about these two little girls having no clothes to wear, I realized that my children's clothes, even though they weren't new, were good enough to wear to school.

I took the last ten dollars, drove to Grant's store, where at that time I was able to purchase two dresses and two pairs of socks for the young girls.

We were the first to arrive at the church that evening. I placed the box addressed to their mother on a shelf over the coat rack. I was in another part of the building when she opened the box. Later that evening I overheard someone say that she had been crying, thanking God for providing school clothes for her daughters. She never knew where the dresses and socks came from. To her it was a miracle from God.

"And the King shall answer and say unto them, Verily, I say unto you, Inasmuch as ye have done it unto one of the least of these my brethren, ye have done it unto me." (Matthew 25:40).

That same week our car broke down and had to be repaired. My husband told the mechanic, "I don't have the money to pay you now. Would you repair the car and accept a small weekly payment?"

The mechanic readily responded, "Don't worry Reverend, I think we can arrange that for you."

The car was repaired and payments were to start the following week. But on Saturday before the first payment was due, I received a call from a new church member. She asked us to come to her home that evening. The call did sound urgent. My husband reluctantly agreed, even though he preferred to stay home and prepare for the Sunday services.

We arrived at this luxurious home. The fireplace was glowing and its warmth invited an atmosphere of relaxation as we sat around and had fellowship. Later we were invited into the dining room for refreshments. After we prayed, the husband who built plazas all over United States gave my husband a check. Thinking it was for our church building fund my husband, without looking at the check said, "Thank you, the church will appreciate this."

Immediately the man answered, "No Pastor, this check is for you. While I was working on a plaza in Indiana, I heard a voice say to me, 'Give your pastor a hundred-dollar check. He is in need.'" We were speechless. The repairs on the car were 96 dollars and the cost of the gas was four dollars. The total expenses came to one hundred dollars even. We were excited, but the couple was also blessed knowing that God used them to bring about our miracle of provision.

We gave our last ten dollars to the Lord gladly, putting our needs last. But God blessed us ten times greater than what we gave. We can never outdo God. While all this was going on, we were hurting financially, but we never stopped doing good. There were times when God provided our basic needs in unexpected ways. One day a church member and her sister, who was not a member, called us to meet them at a store. It was Bond's Men Clothing Store. God touched the heart of the unsaved woman to buy my husband a handsome suit and an expensive coat. A few months later, a man from church also brought my husband a very expensive pair of shoes. These were among some of the many miracles of provision that God gave us.

Several times while ministering on the evangelistic field seeing the financial need of the church pastors, we would take our check and turn it over to them or send them a love gift. How can we close our eyes and pretend we do not see the need?

"Therefore to him that knoweth to do good, and doeth it not, to him it is sin." (James 4:17). James, a servant of the Lord, admonishes the 12 tribes not to boast in making a profit from their buying and selling. He tells them that life is but a vapor that comes and vanishes away. He reminds them that it would be a sin for them to put off until tomorrow the good that could be done today with their profit.

This scripture has been imprinted upon the tablets of my heart since I first memorized it as a young teenager. Throughout the years I have experienced great joy through acts of giving.

The words of the first song I learned in Sunday school were, *"Jesus and others and you, what a wonderful way to spell joy."* If we truly know Jesus and He is first in our lives, we can't help but to do good to others. Secondly, it is His love and compassion that should motivate us to give of ourselves in helping others.

It is wise to ask ourselves the question, *"Why do I give?* What is the motivating factor that makes me give others a helping hand? Is it to be seen and get something back in return? Do I give out of fear, or is it to please God?"

What must our attitude be in giving and doing good?

"Every man according as he purposeth in his heart, so let him give, not grudgingly, or of necessity: for God loveth a cheerful giver." (2 Corinthians 9:7).

"With good will doing service, as to the Lord, and not to men: Knowing that whatsoever good thing any men doeth, the same shall he receive of the Lord, whether he be bond or free." (Ephesians 6:7-8).

Is God aware of our good works, our giving and labor of love?

"For God is not unrighteous to forget your work and labour of love, which ye have shewed toward his name, in that ye have ministered to the saints, and do minister."(Hebrews 6:10). Our good works are not hidden from God.

What will it profit a man if he gains the whole world and loses his soul?

I'm sorry to say, after all our hard labor we cannot take any of our accumulated earthly wealth with us when we leave this world. It's not too late. Release some of your wealth and feed the poor, cloth the naked and house the homeless. Remember the widows, the orphans and the sick. These good deeds are heavenly treasures that we can take with us on that blessed day when we will hear, "Come ye blessed of my Father, inherit the Kingdom prepared for you from the foundation of the world. For I was an hungered, and ye gave me meat: I was thirsty, and ye gave me drink: I was a stranger and ye took me in: Naked, and ye clothed me: I was sick, and ye visited me: I was in prison, and ye came unto me." (Matthew 25:34-36)

As we give with joy, over and over again, and it shall be given to us in abundance. For the measure in which we sow, we shall receive.

He is Always on Time

After our first pastorate in Youngstown, Ohio, we had returned to our home in New York. While we were away our home was rented to a family of five. We found out months later that there were twelve people living in the house. One can just imagine the deplorable condition of our home.

We were faced with no finances to repair the damages. We had to borrow money from our small life insurance policies to make the house livable.

I had the opportunity of going back to my office job at the hospital, but I knew that if I did that, I would not want to move again.

My husband was randomly filling in for pastors, but it was not enough income to pay our bills.

I took on some home sewing to help with the finances, but a few weeks after I started, my sewing machine broke down. We had the life insurance payment to meet that week which was twenty dollars. I said to myself, "The machine is broken. The bill has to be paid. What do I do now?" I had a plaque on the wall above the sewing machine that said, "I can do all things through Christ who strengthens me." I looked up at the verse and I began to cry, "Lord, I cannot do this any longer. I will go back to my office job." At this point, as the scripture verse 1 Peter 5:7 implies, I was casting all my troubles and worries on Him, but I wasn't leaving them there. I was forgetting the second part of the verse, "for He careth for you." For a moment I was allowing worry to take over and forgetting that God is aware of everything that happens in our lives and wants us to turn our troubles and worries over to Him because He cares for us.

I put on my coat, grabbed all the unfinished blouses and walked over to my sister who was in charge of distributing these garments. As I arrived she was outside her home speaking to a woman who was sitting in a car. I brought the garments into her home and went back outside. I was anxious to let her know that I would no longer work for her sewing these garments. I was nervously standing next to my sister, hoping the woman would leave so I could unburden myself. I had my hand in my coat pocket, crunching what I thought was a gum wrapper. Without looking at it, I threw it down on the ground. My sister happened to look down when I did this and said, "Rose, you just dropped a twenty dollar bill." I could not speak. I ran inside her home and began weeping while my sister was still outside talking to the woman.

Where did this twenty-dollar bill come from? I knew it had to be the Lord. But, who put it there? All I could remember was that the night before, at the Wednesday night service, I had hung up my coat on the coat rack. Evidently, God used someone to put the twenty dollars in my coat pocket. This was the exact amount of the life insurance that I had to pay. No one knew about our financial hardship, except our provider, the Lord God. He wanted to reassure me that He would never leave us nor forsake us. He was there all the time! This miracle of provision was the first of several more that followed.

The next morning after returning home from taking my son to school, at my front door there were four large grocery bags of food enough to last us for two weeks. Then a few days later someone left a box with a new suit and raincoat for my youngest son. I was reminded of Psalm 37:25, "I have been young, and now am old; yet have I not seen the righteous forsaken, nor his seed begging bread." and Psalm 23:1, "The Lord is my shepherd; I shall not want."

Several months later, my husband received a call to pastor the Buffalo church. We had to put our house up for sale. A dear Christian woman, hearing about our future move, was interested in purchasing our home. She viewed the house and gave us a large deposit. With this offer we began making plans to move to Buffalo. Just before the sale was finalized, the woman had a change of heart. She didn't want to be away from her children. Here we were almost ready to move and we had to start all over with advertising and showing the home.

Now I'm thinking, "Maybe God doesn't want us to go to Buffalo?" I put the ad in the newspaper again. I began to worry and have mixed feeling about the move. A week later, I went to a Bible study and prayer meeting at the church. I was quietly praying to myself about moving to Buffalo, when a woman who I did not know very well, gave a word of prophecy. The Lord said, *"I am sending you to go forth to minister my Word. I am in control and what happened was for your good. I will go before you, make the way clear and my blessings will be with you."* I was comforted to know that God was concerned about the sale of our home and that He would provide the buyer.

The very first call I received for the sale of the home was from a professor who was teaching at a near by college. They came that same night and walked through the house. They agreed on our price which was better than the first buyers and said, "We will come back later with a deposit." That evening they returned with a fifty-dollar bill and a cake.

My husband looked at me in surprise and said, "We must talk about this. Please excuse us." The first words that he uttered were, "Fifty dollars, we can't give them a binder with only fifty dollars down as a deposit? I don't know what to tell them. They can easily back out of the sale and we may loose another opportunity to sale the home."

I hesitated before responding. Then I said, "They seem to be an honest couple. I know it sounds foolish to accept this offer, but I somehow feel good about it. I feel God is in this. We need to get more information about their financial assets and work income. John, did you notice how hungry they are for the things of God and their many questions? If God brought them there just to save their souls, it will be worth it all, even if the deal falls through." We both agreed to sign the binder and trust God for the rest.

This turned out to be the smoothest sale ever, and most importantly, they both accepted Christ as Lord and Savior. They started to attend our local full gospel church. God was in this transitional period in our lives and brought about three miracles of provision. He never fails. He is always on time!

PART II

The

Mind

(EMOTIONAL)

"For as he thinketh in his heart, so is he."
(Proverbs 23:7)

"Finally, brethren, whatsoever things are true, whatsoever things are honest, whatsoever things are pure, whatsoever things are lovely, whatsoever things are of good report; if there be any virtue, and if there be any praise, think on these things."
(Philippians 4:8)

Chapter Four

MIRACLES OF DELIVERANCE

Deliverance from Suicide

Many answered prayers have come about while spiritual gifts were operating in the church. I personally have witnessed many miracles through the ministering of these gifts. I will share just a couple of attempted suicide situations.

During one of our Wednesday evening services, a young woman came into the service for the first time. One of our assistant pastors was in charge. After the preaching of the Word, he gave an altar call. He asked me to assist him in praying for the needs of the people. This young woman had come up for prayer and was kneeling down at the pew with her head down covering her folded hands. I did not speak to her, but as I was about to put my hand on her shoulder, the Lord gave me a Word of Knowledge to share with her, *"He who taketh his life shall lose it and shall be lost forever. There will be no hope for you beyond the grave, but if you let me come into your heart, I will give you the peace that you are searching for and I will bless you and your home."*

Immediately after hearing this Word of Knowledge, she lifted her head and her arms toward heaven. As she did this, one hand was tightly closed holding a bottle of aspirins. She broke down and cried saying, *"Lord, no one but you knew that I was going to take my life this night if something didn't happen. I'm sorry, Lord. Please forgive me."* At that point I called the Assistant Pastor to pray with me and we led her to the Lord. Her life changed. She received new life through the giver of life, the Lord Jesus and also was healed of hurts. She found the Prince of Peace and love of God that she shared with her husband and child. She went on to accomplish much in her field. of education.

What if the gift, the Word of Knowledge, did not come forth that evening? What if there was no freedom for the Holy Spirit to move in our service? What a tragedy could had occurred, a lost soul, a lost life. *But God* who knows all things loved her enough to reveal the truth to her. By doing so, she received the gift of salvation and her life was spared.

Another incident occurred about the time I went back to college for a degree in art education. While taking a summer course, I met Ann, who had four daughters. Both of us, being older students, became close friends. Because we were taking the same subject at times we studied together at Ann's home. I met her four lovely girls and her husband. The family was very friendly and respectful, but Ann would always blaspheme the name of the Lord. It was so offensive to me that I could not stand there and just listen. I had to defend my faith and my love for God. I asked God, "Please Lord, give me the right words to say to her." I couldn't hold back any longer.

In a low voice I said, "Ann, why do you take the name of God in vain? Instead of cursing you should be thanking Him for giving you a lovely family and a good husband. How can you curse God? It hurts me, but it hurts God more."

Her husband, approving of what I said, stated, "Rose, please tell her. Maybe she will listen to you."

Ann was quiet for a few minutes. Then she looked up at me feeling remorseful and said, "Rose, I'm so sorry. You are right. It's a wonder that my children are good. I'm not a good example to them." After leaving her home, even though I had a love for her family, I had mixed feeling about being with her again. I struggled with the thought of breaking our friendship.

My mother was visiting me the following week. I shared my feelings with her and asked her to visit this family with me. Ann and her family were very happy to meet my mother. It didn't take long for my mother to share the love of Christ with them. They were receptive and demonstrated love toward us, but with some reservations. We said our good-byes and walked down the stairs to my car that was parked in front of their building. Before we drove away, my mother looked up at the second floor where they lived. With a smile upon her face she said, "Rose don't stop your friendship with this family. Continue to share the love of Christ with them. God loves them. Just have patience and be faithful. Only God can bring them to the full understanding of who He is."

I obeyed my mother's spiritual advice and continued my friendship with Ann and her family. She knew my spiritual convictions and respected them. One night I received a call from Ann, "Rose, please can you pray for my daughter Debbie. She overdosed on pills. She tried to take her life." We prayed with her over the phone and followed with a visit to their home.

Debbie was a very attractive young lady who had yielded to a life of promiscuity. She was so bound by a spirit of lust that it affected her self worth and self-esteem, bringing her into a state of depression. But God, who is merciful and forgiving, took her into His arms of love and saved her from self-destruction. Debbie gave her heart to the Lord along with her mother.

On Sunday morning Debbie was in church praising God with us. Not long after her conversion, at a Sunday morning service, Debbie went up for prayer. She was scheduled for a hysterectomy. After we prayed, she went back to her seat crying.

I went over to her and asked, "Debbie, are you okay?"

She said, "I have a lot of pain."

As I prayed with her, the Holy Spirit said, *"She has pain because she is being healed."* After sharing this with her, I told her to go back to her doctor and be re-examined. On Thursday, Debbie was in the doctor's office. After the examination, He said, "I can't understand what happened here. Your reproductive organs are like new. You don't need surgery. This has to be a miracle." Debbie witnessed to the doctor about her healing that took place at church.

Debbie kept her faith in the Lord. She became a worker in the church and a Sunday school teacher. Because of this miracle, God made it possible for her to have children. After her marriage she had a beautiful baby girl, the joy of her life.

This incident brought about three miracles: a deliverance from suicide, salvation and a physical healing.

So many people today are thinking of suicide, even as the women in the above testimonials. They can't deal with their cares and problems. They think that by taking their life, it will all be over. But the sad news is that life does not end here. After death, our souls go to their eternal destination, either to heaven or hell. If one takes his or her life, he or she is lost forever. Thank God, there is a way out, and that is through Jesus Christ, the Son of God, who understands our problems because he loves us. We read in 1 Peter 5:7, "Casting all your care upon him; for he careth for you." He is saying to us, *Come my child, open your heart to me for I love and care about you. You need not struggle with your problems and cares any longer. Bring them to me and lay them at the feet of the cross. Take hold of my hand and we'll walk through life's journey together.*"

These two women who had given up on life, met Jesus and received Him as their Lord and Savior. They turned all their problems over to Him and found new purpose in living. Knowing the giver of life and the Prince of Peace makes life easier and worth living. God once again confirms His Word as we read in Psalm 107:20, "He sent His Word, and healed them, and delivered them from their destructions."

Escape from a Life of Homosexuality

During our ministry I prayed and counseled with several individuals who were involved in or exposed to the homosexual lifestyle. Some were molested at an early age. Others were victimized through the destructive vehicle of pornography that arouses unnatural desires. Because of abuse, a lack of love or neglect, others who had negative images of the opposite sex were drawn into this unnatural lifestyle.

Homosexuality is a subject most people don't want to talk about. Yet those who believe in this practice are out in the forefront of public attention, publicly defending their lifestyle.

I believe God, who created us purposed for a man to have a woman as a soul mate. If God in His unreachable and untouchable wisdom thought for one moment that a man was a better soul mate for Adam, He would have created another man instead of a woman, Eve. This unnatural lifestyle is an affront to God and is contrary to the Word of God.

In Romans 1:24-28 we read, *"Wherefore God also gave them up to uncleanness through the lusts of their own hearts, to dishonour their own bodies between themselves: Who changed the truth of God into a lie, and worshipped and served the creature more than the Creator, who is blessed forever. Amen. For this cause God gave them up unto vile affections: for even their women did change the natural use into that which is against nature: And likewise also the men, leaving the natural use of the woman, burned in their lust one toward another; men with men working that which is unseemly, and receiving in themselves that recompence of their error which was meet. And even as they did not like to retain God in their knowledge, God gave them over to a reprobate mind, to do those things which are not convenient;"*

Another word for reprobate is depraved, which means to be morally bad or corrupt. Because they had chosen to live this lifestyle God turned them over to a corrupt mind.

No matter what the reason may be, none are justifiable in the sight of God. The sin of lustful thoughts takes hold of their minds and members. In denying God's nature, they turn to unnatural practices. Saying that God made them this way, they lie about the truth of God. In my counseling, I found that people who were enticed into this lifestyle still do not have true peace. I'm not surprised! How can one have peace when he or she is living a lie? We read in Proverbs 23:7, "For as he thinketh in his heart, so is he:" But God has news for the homosexual who desires freedom from this lifestyle! God loves the homosexual. He is a precious soul in the sight of God. God prefers not to turn anyone over to a reprobate mind. If they repent and turn from this unnatural lifestyle, God will free the captives and bring peace and deliverance.

The following is an account of a deliverance from a life style of homosexuality. I was invited to attend a day of fasting and praying for specific people and their needs at the home of a church member. Among the other women who were asked to come, there was a woman by the name of Betty. I knew very little about her. She had just started to attend our church with her husband and five children. Betty was going through a time of depression.

After an opening prayer, I felt led by the Holy Spirit to have one of the ladies open the Bible at random and see what God had to say to us. As she opened the Word of God, she began reading in Romans 1:26, which speaks about unnatural affections.

Knowing it was a very delicate subject, immediately I asked the Lord for wisdom and guidance. As I prayed this prayer, the Holy Spirit took over. In obedience I followed His leading.

As we began to pray for Betty, a Word of Knowledge began to come forth through me in a way that I had never experienced before. I closed my eyes and began to see a video of Betty with another woman who was befriending her. With every frame verbal utterances were coming forth from my mouth. I was bringing forth a message from the Lord, when Betty interrupted me saying, "Who told you this. How did you know?"

I told her, "Please, keep your mind on the Lord. He is doing a work in your life today because He loves you."

The video continued and the Lord said, *"The love this woman is giving you is not of me. It is deceitful and unnatural affection sayeth the Lord. Flee from such a one, I say unto thee. For I have come this day to deliver thee and thy household."*

Again the woman looked up at me, crying, and said, "This is true. This woman told me, 'Leave your husband and come stay with me. We will be happy together.' How did you know this?"

I told her, "It is God revealing your life through the Holy Spirit to bring you deliverance."

As the other ladies were still praying, the Holy Spirit began rebuking the spirit of homosexuality that had started to take over her mind. After our prayers, we could see the change in her countenance. She shared that her burden was lifted and her depression had turned into joy. God delivered her from a life of homosexuality and spared her marriage and family. Betty had escaped a life of homosexuality.

Later on, I received an eight-page letter from her thanking me for praying with her. In the letter she wrote that this relationship with the other woman had started at the previous church during a prayer meeting. She thought that the affection being shown by this woman was her way of showing the love of God to her. It didn't end there. The unnatural love was innocently being mistaken for God's pure and holy love.

I have included this part of the letter to reveal how children of God can be deceived and fall into a life of promiscuity. We should be able to discern the difference between a Christian greeting with pure motives and one with immoral intentions. Not all hugs and kisses are holy as Paul the Apostle mentions at the close of many of his writings. Also in Proverbs 27:6 we read, "Faithful are the wounds of a friend, but the kisses of an enemy are deceitful."

The portion of the letter that truly blessed me, was how God had created a greater love between Betty and her husband. As their love for each other and for God grew, they were blessed with another child. They named her Joy because they knew she was a special gift from God. That wasn't all that God did for her family. Today some of her children are serving God in the ministry.

God revealed the truth by uncovering the deceptive spirit of homosexuality that was the cause of her depression.

Through this miracle a woman escaped from a life of homosexuality, and a family unit was preserved. A thousand hours of counseling could never do what our God, the miracle-maker, has done; praise His name! Here again, God works in mysterious ways His wonders to perform! I leave with you Colossians 3:2, 3, 5, "Set your affection on things above, not on things on the earth. For ye are dead, and your life is hid with Christ in God. Mortify therefore your members which are upon the earth; fornication, uncleanness, inordinate affection, evil concupiscence, and covetousness, which is idolatry."

Deliverance from Depression

Many are afflicted today by the mentally debilitating condition called depression. This condition can happen to anyone including Christians. For centuries Christians have used the Word of God as a weapon to battle against stress, anxiety, loneliness, dejection, fear, sadness and low self-esteem. We must hold on to good thoughts: joy, peace, long-sufferings, mercy, love, faith and hope. Our hearts and minds must be saturated with the Word of God. "The troubles of my heart are enlarged: O bring thou me out of my distresses." (Psalm 25:17). "Then they cried unto the Lord in their trouble, and He delivered them out of their distresses." (Psalm 107:6).

At one point in my life, like many, I experienced a short bout of depression due to a heavy overload of stress and anxiety. It happened in Arizona, during a time when my husband was on a rest and recuperation leave following his surgery.

He had just resigned from a very busy pastorate of 15 years due to his health, and he was unable to work. Going from being very busy to being idle, was very difficult on him. It hurt me deeply to see him feel unfulfilled. I kept encouraging him, but at the same time the conditions of our circumstances had become overwhelming.

The only income we had came from my part-time job teaching at a local college. We were suffering financially, and did without many things, but we never complained. We made do with whatever we had. This went on for three years.

After much prayer and waiting upon God my husband recuperated and decided to go into the evangelistic field. At the same time I was offered a full-time teaching position at the college. But rather than accept the job, we decided to move and make our home base in New York.

I was excited about the move. For the first time we would be living within five miles of my son and his family. Within a few weeks after we moved into our home, I believe everything caught up with me. Things were still hard financially. The house we moved into needed so much work. As I began to look at the circumstances I became depressed. I complained to God, "Why, Lord, after leaving all to serve you, why do we find ourselves in this predicament?" I felt that my prayers were not reaching the Lord, and barely reaching the ceiling.

I was wallowing in self-pity. The more I thought about the present circumstances, the weaker I became both mentally and physically. I began losing interest in the things I liked to do. Anyone who knew me could tell you how much I loved my grandchildren. It was obvious that something was drastically wrong when I had no desire to see them. I couldn't cook, do housework or even watch television. All I did was lie on the couch.

My husband tried to give me words of encouragement. Knowing how much I enjoyed watercolors, he tried to get me interested in painting, but nothing seemed to interest me. I tried to tell him, *"John, you don't understand. My mind is like a sieve. I can't hold on to anything."*

I knew from my experience in praying for others whom had this condition that my mind was now in a state of depression. This condition not only tries to control your mind, but it drains all your strength. I wanted deliverance, but I just couldn't help myself. I recall begging God, *"Please, Lord, after serving you all these years, don't let me lose my mind. Please God, deliver me and set me free."*

That same afternoon, I was lying on the couch and I heard a voice within me say, *"Turn the television on."* I hadn't turned the television on since we had moved to New York. In my condition, I had lost all desire to watch television. I didn't even know what programs were scheduled. Within myself I said, *"I don't want to watch television!"*

I just ignored what I was hearing. But within minutes, I heard the voice again, loud and demanding, *"Turn the television on!"* This time I listened. With the little strength that I had, I turned the television on and the 700 Club program was in progress. My first thought was, "Turn it off. It's just another program."

As I went to turn the program off, Ben and Pat were praying. I heard Ben who had a *Word of Knowledge* say, *"There is a woman out there lying on a couch. I don't know how to say this, but her mind is like a sieve. She can't hold on to anything."* For a moment I froze in amazement. I could hardly believe what I heard! I literally jumped off the couch, put my face up against the television screen as Ben was praying. Wanting so desperately to be delivered, I immediately accepted the Word of Knowledge for my deliverance.

All I could think about was, *"God, you must really love me enough to give Ben the exact words. Lord, I thank you that, even though I could not reach you, you cared enough to reach down to me.*" God touched me as I prayed with Ben. A surge of strength invaded my body, and the joy of the Lord was restored in my mind and spirit. Through that prayer I received my miracle of deliverance from depression.

Going through this experience has helped me to better understand the debilitating affects of depression. On different occasions, when I gave my testimony, several men and women were touched and delivered of depression. I learned a personal lesson through this trying time. When a troubling situation arises, I need to keep my eyes on the Lord, not on the circumstance. The way I handled that circumstance had opened the door to self-pity and dejection. Satan had deceived me for a moment, but God delivered me and restored my joy.

Another very painful and sad situation happened to one of our youth while ministering in Youngstown, Ohio. Jim had gone away to college in California and was living with his Uncle Ted. His uncle, a college professor, had a lovely home near a cliff overlooking the ocean. Prior to Jim leaving Ohio, he seemed to be a well-adjusted reserved young man who loved the Lord.

While living in California, Jim joined a church and was active in several programs. All seemed to be going well for him. But one day Uncle Ted arrived home early, and as usual he was looking for Jim. Jim was nowhere to be found. His uncle realized this was unusual and immediately went outdoors looking for him. As Uncle Ted was going to his car, he happened to glance over at the cliff near his house. He noticed a man standing right at the edge of the cliff. Ted realized it was Jim. Immediately he ran towards the cliff and called out, "Jim, Jim, it's Uncle Ted. I was worried about you." Jim did not move or speak. He just stood there at the edge of the cliff, looking downward. His uncle, knowing this was an unpredictable and precarious situation, pleaded with Jim, "Please, Jim, move back from the cliff. I'm here for you. We can talk." Finally after some persuasion Jim went back to the house with his Uncle Ted.

Jim had contemplated jumping off the cliff. His uncle tried to communicate with him, but he would not respond or speak and isolated himself from the family. The uncle realized that this behavior was not normal for Jim. Something was seriously wrong. He decided to take Jim back to his mother in Ohio.

The very night Jim arrived home, my husband and I were called to go and pray for him. My heart broke when I saw this fine handsome young man overtaken with a destructive spirit of depression and suicide. He was lying on the bed staring at the wall with his back toward us. His hands were gripping the sides of the mattress. He would not talk or look at any of us. He didn't open his mouth to eat or drink. We prayed, but nothing happened. The family had called 911 for an ambulance. He was transported to a receiving hospital.

I told the Lord we were not going to give up and see this young man stay in that state of mind. In the past we had experiences dealing with similar situations and we knew what we had to do. Our church people were all in prayer for Jim. My husband and I visited him in the hospital several times. We reassured him, "Jim, God is with you. He loves you and will deliver you from this."

After we prayed with him, he began to open up, but with a loud voice he said, "I hate my father. Why did he leave me when I needed him. I'll never forgive him. I hate him! Why did he leave me? Why did God allow this?" There was anger and bitterness in his voice. We shared with Jim that God wants us to forgive. He was so upset and then he closed up again. We had thanked God that he opened up, even if it was just to let us know what was troubling him. That was the first time he had shared this with anyone.

All these hurts that were causing his depression were bottled up inside him. Finally he was able to express them verbally. The chains of despair, the hurt and the dejection had oppressed him in body, mind and spirit. Several stressful events had brought on his depression. One was starting college thousands of miles away from home. He was separated from his mother, the only parent he had. The new environment and living with his uncle might have renewed the deep hurt he felt about the absence of his own natural father. Overtaken by feelings of low self-esteem, he became a prisoner to a debilitating state of mind called depression.

I called his mother and a few ladies to join me in praying and fasting for Jim. We all gathered in one mind and one accord. God gave one of the ladies the passage of scripture that talks about deliverance from an evil spirit. These spirits only come out through prayer and fasting. We had the power of the written Word, and coupled it with fasting and prayer. The anointing of the Holy Spirit and power fell upon us. We took the authority according to the scriptures and rebuked the spirit of darkness out of Jim's life and mind. We claimed his soul, mind and body back to God His creator.

After praying this prayer, we all sensed in our spirit that something had happened.

Just before we departed, Jim's mother got a phone call from the hospital, saying," Come, you can take your son home. We don't know what happened during the last two hours, but Jim is fine. A complete change came over him. He has been talking and he wants to come home. He's not the same young man who was admitted here a couple of weeks ago. You must see him for yourself. It has to be a miracle!" She told them that we were praying for Jim during the last two hours.

That evening my husband and I visited Jim at his home. I can not put into words the overwhelming joy we all were experiencing. We knelt down in prayer. Jim prayed side by side with us, offering thanks to God for the miracle of deliverance from all his past hurts.

Jim continued to serve the Lord. He later married and has a family of his own. Another life was delivered and snatched from the hands of the enemy of our soul through the power of prayer and fasting. To God be the Glory; great things He has done!

As human beings, God created us with physical, emotional and spiritual abilities. In simplified words we are made up of body, mind and spirit. Depression can have an affect on any one or more of the three components. For this reason many times the origin of the depression goes undetected. Depression may be only a temporary condition. It can be triggered by one of several different life experiences. A simple change like moving to a new residence, losing a job or experiencing a more stressing experience such as the death of a loved one may bring it on. When depression continues without recognizable cause, there is reason for concern. If depression becomes major, it will affect the normal functioning of the physical, emotional and sometimes spiritual aspects of the person.

In some cases there are one or two stages of mental illness that may precede depression.

1. *The first stage is OBSESSION*: Obsession may be the starting point and basic underlining cause of depression. The generally accepted definition of obsession is preoccupation with a troublesome thought. Continuously dwelling upon any troubling thought starts to attract other negative thoughts. If they are not destroyed when reaching this first stage in the mental process, they will take root and begin to oppress the mind. A good example of this is a seed. It is planted in the ground. The seed will take root and germinate as it is fed by the elements of the earth: water, sunlight and soil. If it is not fed by these elements, it will dry up and die. The seed can symbolize an obsession. If the negative thought is not fed, it will die. In this case, the obsession can be a temporary condition and will last for only a short period of time.

2. The *second stage is OPPRESSION*: Now the troubling thought has multiplied and has advanced to a more controlling stage called oppression. The thoughts begin to weigh heavily on the mind. When levels of stress and anxiety increase, mental distress and limited physical function occur. This second stage takes over our thinking ability. Some of the symptoms that may start to manifest in this stage are loss of sleep, losing one's joy, poor appetite and low self-esteem. If this state of the mind continues to be preoccupied with negative

thoughts, and at this point no deliverance has occurred, the person may become a victim of depression.

What is depression? It is a state of mind that causes a person to become depressed. They are discouraged with life, feeling dejected, usually accompanied with a feeling of hopelessness, self-doubt and lethargy. A considerable decrease in normal activity occurs. Coping with the normal routine of life becomes difficult. The depressed person withdraws from society.

There are underlining causes that bring a person into a state of depression. There are basic mental conditions that a person may experience that can lead to depression. Let us look at some of the causes and effects of depression.

What causes people to become depressed?

A sudden tragedy
Loss of a loved one, a job, finances
Guilt or unforgiveness
Built-up anger due to a hurt
Feeling of hopelessness
Dejection
Loneliness
Chemical imbalance

What does depression affect?

Body, mind and the spirit

How does it affect the body?

Lack of sleep or oversleeping
Loss of appetite or overeating
Loss of energy

How does depression affect the mind?

Low self-esteem

Interferes with decision-making
Inability to concentrate
Fixation of the mind
Suicidal tendencies
Feelings of helplessness
Feelings of guilt
Low self-worth
Always saddened

How does depression affect the spirit?

Blocks the joy of the Lord
Blocks the peace of God
Blocks God out of one's mind

If the cause of the depression is diagnosed as a biological chemical imbalance, medical science can help. But in many cases the underlining deep-rooted cause needs more than scientific medication. For deliverance and permanent recovery it needs a prescription that will medicate the three parts of the person: body, mind and spirit. This is called miracle medication. This kind of prescription is good for all types of depression. The spiritual ingredients are prayer, faith and sometimes fasting. The results are peace, joy and freedom.

Our minds are so fragile. God creates in us the ability to think. We are responsible for what we allow ourselves to think about. The mind is a battlefield. It is made up of receptors, receiving stimuli from good and evil forces. When we receive these messages, they create positive or negative thoughts. These messages come from things we hear, see or experience. Therefore, there is a sifting process that takes place in the mind. We must hold onto that which is good and separate it from that which is harmful or evil.

Paul gave to the church at Philippi a good anti-depression prescription. It is a prescription that keeps the body, mind and spirit healthy. "Finally, brethren, whatsoever things are true, whatsoever things are honest, whatsoever things are just, whatsoever things are pure, whatsoever things are lovely, whatsoever things are of good report; if there be any virtue, and if there be any praise, think on these things." (Philippians 4:8).

Our minds are exposed to both good and evil everyday. We need to safeguard against negative thoughts by filling our minds with all the positive things mentioned above.

PART III

The

Spirit

(GOD CONSCIOUSNESS)

"And the Lord God formed man of the dust of the ground,
and breathed into his nostrils the breath of life;
and man became a living soul."
(Genesis 2:7)

"Howbeit when He the Spirit of truth, is come, he will guide you into
all truth: for he shall not speak of himself; but whatsoever he shall
hear, that shall he speak: and he will shew you things to come."
(John 16:13)

Chapter Five

MIRACLES OF SALVATION

Ready to Witness

Witnessing can take place anywhere, any place and anytime. When we witness to someone, our spirit should be attentive to the leading of the Holy Spirit. For God knows the heart of a person and He can give us the words that will touch that individual.

I have heard some Christians say, "Well, I don't have to speak to the unsaved about the Lord. They can know Him by the life I lead." Yes, it is important that we live a godly life, but that in itself cannot save anyone. What Paul spoke to the Romans still applies to us today, "For whosoever shall call upon the name of the Lord shall be saved. How then shall they call on him in whom they have not believed? And how shall they believe in him of whom they have not heard? And how shall they hear without a preacher (also refers to us)?"(Romans 10:13-14), and "So then faith cometh by hearing, and hearing by the word of God." (Romans 10:17). Many Christians rub shoulders with the unsaved every day, and yet they never feel the urgency to tell them about the saving power of our Lord and Savior or share their own testimony with them. Others will say, "I can't witness; I'm afraid of what they may say." 2 Timothy 1:7 states, "For God hath not given us the spirit of fear; but of power, and of love, and of a sound mind."

Fear is not of God. It is a deterrent that Satan uses to keep you from witnessing.

Others will say, "I'm ashamed to approach someone and start witnessing. What will they think of me?" Mark 8:38 states "Whosoever therefore shall be ashamed of me and of my words in this adulterous and sinful generation; of him also shall the Son of man be ashamed, when he cometh in the glory of his Father with the holy angels." Romans 1:16 states, "For I am not ashamed of the gospel of Christ: for it is the power of God unto salvation to every one that believeth; to the Jew first and also to the Greek." How can we hold back and keep to ourselves the good message of salvation and our personal testimony?

Early one morning before the dawn of day, the Holy Spirit impressed me with a parable relating to everyday life that illustrates a spiritual truth. It was time to go shopping for a new vacuum cleaner. At the store there were two salespersons working in that department. After looking over the different models, we found one that we liked, but we had to learn more about its features. One of the salespeople gave us a limited description of the vacuum cleaner. But the other salesperson interrupted and said, "I have the same model at home and let me tell you it is wonderful! I have five children, a dog and a cat, and believe me, after I vacuum my floors you could never tell that I have so much traffic. If you buy this vacuum cleaner, you will never be sorry. I know because I have experienced firsthand what this vacuum cleaner can do. I would highly recommend it to anyone." Did we buy that vacuum cleaner? We most certainly did, without hesitation.

This parable illustrates that, if we first have a personal relationship with God through Jesus and the Holy Spirit, we are unable to conceal it and keep it to ourselves. Just as the salesperson, with fervency, couldn't help but tell us how great her vacuum cleaner worked, likewise we should have the same burning desire to share the Word of God and our testimony to the lost.

How can the unbeliever know unless they hear the message of salvation? It is the living Word of God that can change the sinful nature of mankind and make us a new creature in Christ Jesus. For it is only by the blood that Jesus shed at Calvary that people can be forgiven of their sins and be reconciled to God the Father through Christ.

Jesus said in John 14:6, "I am the way, the truth, and the life: no man cometh unto the Father, but by me." Romans 10:9 states "If thou shalt confess with thy mouth the Lord Jesus, and shalt believe in thine heart that God hath raised him from the dead, thou shalt be saved." In 1 John 1: 8-9, we read, "If we say that we have no sin, we deceive ourselves, and the truth is not in us. If we confess our sins, He is faithful and just to forgive us our sins, and to cleanse us from all unrighteousness."

As His witnesses we are commissioned to take His Word to the uttermost parts of the world. It is a good idea to start at home first, then branch out to others we encounter in our daily life.

Scripture tells us in 2 Corinthians 5:20 that we are His ambassadors to spread the glad news that Jesus loves everyone and died to redeem them. Luke 14:23 states "And the Lord said unto the servant, go out into the highway and hedges and compel them to come in, that my house may be filled."

We must go and gently compel the unsaved to come into the fold while it is still day, for the night will come when no man can work. I believe the hour will soon come when all doors for witnessing will be closed before our very eyes. I often wonder if God will hold us responsible in that day when we stand before His presence. Will He say, "Where are the sheep that you have brought into the fold?" Think about the many opportunities you had to witness and share your testimony with the unbelievers, but you let them go by.

If we can only realize that there is a living soul within each individual who will one day stand before the judgment seat of God, and He will issue their sentence; will it be heaven or hell for eternity?

What better gift can we bring to the Lord than to win souls into the kingdom when one soul is worth more then the whole world to Him. *"God give us a burden to win the lost!"* There is no greater joy then when a soul comes to the Lord. Even the angels in heaven rejoice over every soul that comes into the kingdom.

The strong interest to witness started in my teenager years. At my church, I was taught about witnessing through the Word of God. By nature, I was a shy person and certainly not forward, but in spite of my shyness and lack of witnessing knowledge, I still had a desire to witness. The only exposure I had was giving out tracts at a street corner and asking people, "Do you want to be saved?"

This method of witnessing did not seem to be productive in winning souls into the kingdom. For me it was embarrassing standing there for an hour, and yet not one soul was won to the Lord. We were told that we should not be ashamed of the Gospel. It wasn't a matter of being ashamed because my desire to witness superceded my shyness. The problem was not knowing how to witness, where to witness and when to witness.

As I matured in the ways of the Lord, I realized that the Holy Spirit, my teacher and coach, was teaching me how to witness. He will teach us if we listen, obey and follow His leading. In doing so, He will give us the words to say at the right time and in the right way. Who knows best the heart of man, but the Lord.

Are you equipped and ready to witness to the hungry soul? Do you know the salvation scriptures or have you memorized them? Are you ready to share your personal testimony? When witnessing you never know what questions you will be asked. Knowing that every situation will be different, it is important to rely on the Word of God and the Holy Spirit for your answers.

Every day, anywhere you must be ready to witness for the Lord to a lost and dying world without Christ. You must first have a desire to witness. Then pray for the empowerment of the Holy Spirit to give you boldness in sharing the Word and your testimony to a needy, adulterous and sinful generation.

My First Witnessing Experience

The deep desire to share my relationship and love I had for Jesus lingered with me. It was foremost in my prayers. In church we would sing that beautiful hymn, *"Lord, lay some soul upon my heart, and win that soul to thee."* In my prayers, I would repeat the words to this song.

The Lord heard my prayer. I was in my early twenties, when I had my first witnessing experience. We met June at her aunt's home. She worked as a model. Before I knew it, we were engaged in a conversation. June did not waste any time bringing up the subject of religion.

She asked me, "Rose, do you believe in God in the same way my aunt does?" With this leading question I wondered if June had a personal encounter with the Lord.

Without hesitation I said, "Yes, I do June, but let me tell you why I not only believe in God but also in Jesus the Son of God, who is the only one that can forgive our sins."

June quickly replied, "When I go to church with my parents we confess our sins to the priest. Then we have to do a penance in order for us to be forgiven."

I quoted John 14:6 and said, "June, Jesus is the only one who was given the authority by God to forgive our sin and we can only go to God through Jesus who is our mediator. Jesus, who was without sin, paid the price for our sins on the cross. We do not have to do penance to receive forgiveness of our sins. Jesus said, "If we confess our sins (to Him, not to man), He is faithful and just to forgive us our sins, and to cleanse us from all unrighteousness." (1 John 1:9).

After hearing this, her understanding was enlightened by the truth of God's Word. She gladly accepted Christ as her Savior. This was the first and last encounter I had with June.

However, many years later, her aunt heard that my husband was scheduled to hold meetings in her area. She called and invited us to her home for fellowship. While there, with excitement in her voice she said, "Rose, I don't know if you recall witnessing to my niece June. She told me how you led her to the Lord many years ago. I want you to know that she has been serving the Lord ever since." When I heard this, I was happy and speechless. It had been my first witnessing experience. I felt so humbled to think that God had answered my prayer and used me to win my first soul into His kingdom.

Witnessing Can Be Part of Everyday Life

After this first experience, witnessing became a part of my everyday life. It would take volumes to record every one. This chapter recounts some of my various witnessing situations. You will find some of these situations to be unique because of the way they happened. They are all witnessing experiences that have happened in my life. As an ambassador for Christ, you too can experience the joy of winning a soul to the Lord. First ask God to give you a burden for souls, then allow the Holy Spirit to guide you. As you read these miracles of Salvation I trust that you will be challenged to say, "Lord, I want to be a witness and bring souls with me into the kingdom. Teach me how Holy Spirit."

A Blind Man Finds Christ

One day after making a hospital call, Mrs. Moore and I had stopped for a quick lunch. Before leaving the restaurant as we were waiting in line to pay for our meals, I shared with Mrs. Moore that I felt impressed by the Lord to witness to the blind man who was standing in the line in front of us. We followed him to his car and tapped on the driver's window. As the driver looked towards us, he hesitantly rolled down the window. I started by telling the blind passenger, "Sir, we have a message for you."

The driver at first became upset and annoyed by us and said to the blind man in an excitable voice, "Don't pay any attention to them. Let's go."

The blind man answered the driver, "It's okay Harry, I want to hear what these ladies have to say. My name is Bill. Please tell me the message."

"Bill, Jesus gave us a message for you. He wants you to know how much He cares for you and that He loved you enough to die for you so that one day you can spend eternity with Him in heaven." Harry's attitude began to change toward us as he listened to the message. As we spoke tears were brought to the blind man's eyes. Bill was blinded both physically and spiritually. Bill and Harry both accepted the Lord.

He is no longer blind spiritually, for the miracle of salvation opened his eyes to the truth of God's Word. We said, "Bill, you had the most important healing today, the healing of the soul that prepares you for heaven, where there is no physical sickness. This same Jesus you accepted into your heart can also heal your physical blindness as He did in Bible days and still heals the blind today."

With a joyful voice Bill said, "I'm so thankful that you cared enough to tell us about Jesus. I had given up on life and I didn't want to live any longer, but I can't explain what happened after you prayed.

Now I feel different, like something good is going to happen in my life."

Before leaving, Mrs. Moore said, "Sir, if you don't have a church of your own, we invite you to visit our church. We'll be praying for you. God bless you."

Jim, the Window Washer

Another witnessing situation occurred when Jim, the window washer, came to our home. I had visitors at my house while he was washing the windows. I excused myself from them to write a check out for Jim, when I heard the Holy Spirit say, "Give this man a Bible."

At first I thought, "What will Jim think if I give him a Bible? He'll probably refuse it or already has one." Knowing that it was my flesh speaking, I decided to obey the Holy Spirit.

I began witnessing to Jim about the saving grace of our Lord and Savior. Then I gave him one of my favorite Bibles. I quickly wrote some scriptures on the first page with a note, "God loves you, Jim. We will be praying for you."

With joy he accepted the Bible and said, "This is something! I can't believe it! You're giving me one of your favorite Bibles, wow! I've never had a Bible before, and I haven't gone to church since I was a little boy." After I witnessed to him, he made a commitment to the Lord and asked me, "Where is your church? I want to come and bring my family."

What an opportunity I would have missed out on if I had listened to my flesh rather then the Holy Spirit.

Jim is only one out of so many people who are hungry and thirsty for the Word of God. We have the spiritual food that they need and yet we bypass them every day, never caring or sharing the living water and the bread of life that they so desperately need. When we have a love and a burden for the lost souls, we can't help but share Christ with them.

A Magazine Article Brought Tears

We were at our first full-time ministry at Youngstown, Ohio. I was washing some clothes at a Laundromat and while waiting, I picked up an issue of *Life* magazine to read. The article was about an Olympic skier who we will call Jane. She was badly injured while skiing, leaving her paralyzed. As I read about her tragic accident, tears began rolling down my cheeks.

It isn't unusual in our daily life to read or hear about tragic accidents, but there was something different about this article that moved me with an overwhelming compassion that invaded my spirit. I couldn't put the magazine down. I felt the Holy Spirit urging me to write to Jane and share encouraging words of comfort and the message of salvation. The only address mentioned in the *Life* magazine was the name of the town, the state and her full name but no street or box number.

That same night, after everyone went to sleep, I sat at my desk and began writing. The first thought that came to me was "How do you write to a total stranger?" Then I thought, "She may be a stranger to me, but certainly not a stranger to God."

I began the letter by sharing the compassion that God gave me for her as I read about the accident, causing me to shed teardrops staining the very article I was reading.

I told her how much God loved her and was concerned about her sufferings and disappointments. Step by step as the Holy Spirit led me, I shared the Word of God and message of salvation. "No matter what we go through, the most important issue in life is to know that we are ready to meet the Lord. Only Jesus can comfort you and bring peace and joy into your life. Find a good Bible teaching church in your area. I have enclosed some gospel literature to help you in your walk with the Lord. We'll be praying for you."

Within a few weeks, I received a letter back from her, telling me, "You will never know how much your letter meant to me." She told me she had accepted the Lord and was looking for a church. She went on to say, "Please send me some photos of your family and yourself with some information about your ministry." I was so happy in my spirit that I could barely sleep that night, thanking God that I obeyed the leading of the Holy Spirit to write to Jane.

Later that week I wrote back to her. Knowing that she was a babe in Christ, I enclosed more gospel literature along with the photos she requested and a summary of our ministry. I sent the letter to the same address as the first one. To my amazement, the letter returned to me, "no such address." I resent the same letter and it came back again post marked, "no such address."

I must admit that I was very disappointed wondering, "What if she thinks I didn't want to answer her letter? If only I could tell her what happened." I was feeling badly about not being able to reach her, but when I prayed, I was convinced that I had completed my part in Jane's salvation. I prayed daily for her and I remember telling the Lord, "Maybe someday I will meet her, if not here on earth, I will see her in heaven."

About four years later, while ministering in Buffalo, New York, I was speaking on witnessing to a group of women. I shared this wonderful testimony with the ladies about how God can use a simple magazine article as a vehicle of communication to win a soul. A few weeks later, while I was at the church, I received a call from Mrs. Moore, my prayer partner.

She was all excited, "Sister Franco, I am listening to a radio program from the Full Gospel Business Men's Convention in California. A woman by the name of Jane is giving her testimony of how she came to the Lord. She said that a woman wrote to her about the Lord and hopes that someday she will meet her in person. I think she is talking about you! Please turn the radio on."

I looked around the church office for a radio, but I was unable to find one. However, hearing this good news, I immediately went on my knees and thanked God for allowing me to have a little part in her salvation. Who can understand how, where and what vehicle God will use as a means to save a soul—even a simple thing like a magazine made with paper and ink translated in words a tragic life story. All the Lord needed to bring life into this article was for one of His children to act upon the leading of the Holy Spirit.

Don't Throw the Church Bulletin Away

Another witnessing situation had to do with a church bulletin. Never throw your church bulletin away! Try using it as a witnessing tool. Extend an invitation to someone to attend your church by introducing your beliefs and announcements via the bulletin. Let me tell you what I do with my church bulletins.

While we were at a church for both morning and evening services, we went out for lunch with the pastor and his wife. While waiting for the pastor in the entrance of the restaurant, I looked over at a family that was waiting to be seated. Then I heard the Holy Spirit say, "Take the church bulletin and invite those people to the evening service." Remembering that I had put the bulletin in my purse, I immediately obeyed the move of the Holy Spirit before my carnal self had time to give me every reason why I shouldn't go. I very gently went over to them, and with a friendly smile and the love of the Lord, I greeted them and introduced myself.

I followed by sharing about the wonderful church we were at that morning, and I extended an invitation for them to join us in the evening service. I gave them the bulletin with the church address; they openly accepted it without any reservation. The son read through the bulletin and said, "I accept your invitation, but my family and I have an appointment this evening, but thank you for the invite."

Then his mother, who was with them, read the bulletin and said, "Oh, I know where that church is; I will try to come for the evening service."

I responded by saying, "I will look for you." She thanked me again for inviting them.

That evening when the service had started I did not see the woman in church, but my heart was telling me that she would be coming. Without drawing any attention to myself, I kept an eye out for her. About 15 minutes into the service, who do you think entered the sanctuary? Yes, it was the woman from the restaurant. I was so happy to see her. She came and sat next to me and said, "I am so happy you invited me to this church."

During the salvation call, without any coaching, she turned to me and said, "I want Jesus to come into my heart. What should I do?" After sharing some scriptures with her and telling her that Jesus loved her and died for her, she asked me, "Will you come up to the altar with me, I want to accept Jesus." Weeping with joy she accepted Christ as her Savior and started to attend that church.

Another soul was won into the kingdom and who knows if her family followed! All because of an invitation given by way of a church bulletin coupled with God's love demonstrated through a friendly smile.

There have been times when I have left the bulletin in the ladies room, or on a serving table, or with a waitress as I shared Christ with her. One never knows who may be in a desperate situation and might pick up that bulletin and be encouraged to attend church or even make a phone call. Knowingly or unknowingly, you might have planted a seed in winning a soul to the Lord by the Christ-like impression that you made in their life. It may be through a smile, a helping hand, a church bulletin, an encouraging word, a phone conversation or a business transaction. All these things can be the underlining cause that leads to the salvation of a soul.

Prayer during a Turbulent Flight

On one of my trips from New York to California, a young medical student was sitting in the plane next to me. She sat there very quietly reading a textbook. I was busy writing a new chapter for my book. On and off the young woman would glance in my direction. It soon became obvious to me that she was curious or interested in what I was writing. Realizing this, I silently prayed, "Holy Spirit, if I am to share Christ with her, please give me the words that will open her heart to listen."

No sooner had I prayed this prayer then the young woman turned to me and said something about our turbulent flight. Knowing her concern, I said, "I always pray when this happens. Would you like to pray with me?"

She was very frightened by the turbulence and said, "Please, anything that will help!" We prayed a simple prayer of protection. As soon as I finished praying, the turbulence stopped and the young woman looked at me in amazement. "It really stopped. Wow, I can't believe that happened." I told her that if we pray in the Name of Jesus, God will hear and answer our prayers because of His love for us.

With this, I introduced Jesus as a friend, a comforter who would always be with her. She looked at me and said, "I went to church as a little girl, but I really never knew much about God and religion. My parents have not gone to church for years. I believe in the power of the mind, and as long as I do good, I'm all right." Even though she said this, I could sense there was a hunger for the truth.

I told her about some of my own personal experiences. "As an art teacher, I had achieved some acclaim in the field of art, but nothing could ever compare with the joy, peace and contentment I have found in Jesus. Knowing Jesus Christ as my personal Savior supercedes any and all of my earthy accomplishments. For these are all temporal, but the things of God are eternal." Seeing that she was interested in the miracle I was writing about, I shared with her how God had miraculously delivered my son and I from a near fatal car accident and healed my body.

All she could say was, "That is amazing!"

She was absorbing every word that came out of my mouth and said, "Please, explain how I can experience this peace and joy in my own life. I've had some disappointments in my life, and at times I feel so helpless and alone. I have no one that I can talk to as a friend."

The door was wide open. All I had to do was introduce her to her new friend Jesus. She had little tears falling from her eyes. She confessed Christ, asked His forgiveness and promised to follow the Lord. I asked if she had a Bible. She said, "No, but I will buy one." I told her to begin reading the book of John in the New Testament and to start attending a good Bible-teaching church where she could learn more about the Word of God and have the fellowship that she so needed. With excitement in her voice she said, "Yes, I will do that because I want to learn more about God and the Bible." I told her I would be praying for her as we went our separate ways.

Do you leave God and your testimony at home when taking a plane trip? Think upon these words when you take your next trip.

More Than a Crab Cake Dinner

Would you ever think about witnessing to someone in a restroom? I agree, it does sound a little unusual. Let me tell you what happened.

We were in Maryland ministering at an Assembly of God church. The Pastor invited us for dinner at a restaurant near the waterfront specializing in fish dinners. We were driving our own car, following the pastor and his wife.

The restaurant was about 35 miles away. As we were driving, my husband had second thoughts about going so far out of the way because we had to travel to another city for the evening service. But I felt badly about disappointing the pastor, so we decided to stay for dinner, and I'm glad we did.

I had my favorite Maryland stuffed-crab patties. Before dessert I excused myself and went to the ladies room. There were four ladies in the restroom, so I had to wait my turn. While waiting, I felt the urge to speak to them. Somehow I started by saying how much I enjoyed the crab cakes and how fortunate they were to live near this great seafood restaurant.

One of the ladies said, "We do not live here. We are from Annapolis."

With this I picked up the conversation by saying, "We were in Annapolis this morning speaking at a wonderful church, in fact we are having dinner here with the pastor and his wife. Do you attend any church?"

"No, but we have been thinking about starting to go to church." Then I shared the salvation message and told them the Lord loved them and wanted to give them peace and joy. They were very hungry to know more about Jesus.

I invited them to come to our table and meet the pastor from the Annapolis church. They excitedly followed me and acted like little children about to receive a prize. The prize they each received was the gift of eternal life. After introducing them to the pastor, together we prayed for them, and at the end of the prayer they each accepted the Lord as their Savior. Then they told the pastor, "We want to come to your church. Please give us the address."

Was it worth traveling 35 miles to that restaurant? Did God know that the four women would be there at the same time? Did the Lord know that I would obey the wooing of the Holy Spirit to speak to these strange women in a restaurant restroom and by introducing them to the pastor that they would receive Christ? I believe this was all in God's plan. It pays to obey the Holy Spirit. The rewards are great. Four new souls were added to the kingdom of God.

Over a Cup of Coffee

I met a woman at the hospital while my husband was having some tests done. My son John, who was with us said, "Mom, instead of waiting here, why don't you go to the cafeteria, relax and have a cup of coffee. I'll stay with Dad and join you later" John walked me to the cafeteria.

A woman was sitting alone at the only table available. I asked her, "Miss, do you mind sharing your table?"

"No, not at all. Please sit down. My name is Ellen."

It was obvious that she had been crying. She told me that her son was in a car accident and was critically ill. She said, "I don't know what to do. They want to send my son home from the hospital. He is going to need a lot of care. I have other children at home and I don't feel I can handle everything!"

"Ellen, maybe your church can give you a helping hand."

"Rose, we do not go to any church. We have always been too busy working or involved with sports."

"The Bible tells us that as parents, we are responsible to teach and raise our children in the ways of the Lord. It is important that we make time and go with them to a Bible teaching church where together we can learn about God as a family."

I witnessed to her about the saving and healing power of Jesus. She broke down and cried as I shared the Word of God with her. She openly confessed Christ and accepted Him into her heart. I reassured her that now she was not alone. The Lord would be walking with her through her son's recovery.

With a repented heart she said, "I have failed my children by not taking them to church all those years. I hoped it isn't too late. Where is your church? I want to come there."

"We do not pastor a church. We speak in different churches, but I can recommend one in your area."

"Rose, my family and I will start attending church. There has always been an emptiness in our lives. Now I know why."

Minutes later, my son came down to the cafeteria and gave me the good news that my husband did not need surgery because the doctor said the growth in his kidney that they had seen in the x-ray was gone. Praise God! This is a good example of what can happen when we take care of God's business. While I was witnessing to this woman, God was performing a miracle for my husband.

She Never Told Me about Jesus!

Did you ever think of witnessing to someone sitting near you while traveling on a bus? I did. My grandson David, 10 years of age at the time, and I were traveling on a bus going from New York to Albany. As usual I wanted David to sit with me, but all the seats were taken, so we had to sit across from each other. Sitting next to me was a young college student going to a camp in upstate New York to work as a counselor. When she shared this with me, at first I thought it was a Christian camp that I was familiar with, but in the course of our conversation I realized it was a secular camp.

I first listened to Ruth talking about her family and her major in school, and then she began questioning me about my background. I told her about my secular teaching job as a starting point to draw some interest. I followed by saying, "My most important activity is ministering to the young people in my church."

Ruth asked, "What do you mean by ministering?"

"I share with the young people the living Word of God and they apply it to their everyday lives."

Again she responded, "What is the living Word of God?"

"The Bible is the living Word of God. Men through the inspiration of God and the Holy Spirit wrote the words. Every answer to the needs of life is in the Bible."

The young woman was not raised in a church and had never owned a Bible. This was all new to her. Her eyes were wide open, and her heart was hungry to learn more about this book called the Bible.

In this situation it was important for me to explain why Jesus the Son of God took upon Himself the sins of mankind. He died and arose again and now sits at the right hand of God interceding on our behalf. Since she had no religious background, the Holy Spirit led me to share the purpose of reading the Bible.

I explained that the Bible is your guidepost to teach you how to live a life pleasing to God and it prepares you for heaven. In Psalms 119:11 we find "Thy Word have I hid in mine heart, that I might not sin against thee." Psalms 119:105 states "Thy Word is a lamp unto my feet, and a light unto my path."

She said, "I never heard anything like this before. I have a friend who says she is a so-called Christian, but she never told me anything about God or Jesus. I don't understand why she would keep this from me. I'm so happy you sat next to me and shared these wonderful things about God and the Bible. I want to know more; what shall I do?" We prayed the Sinner's Prayer and asked Jesus to bless her life and use her as a witness for His glory. She was bubbling over with joy and asked for a Bible. I promised her that I would send her one. We said our good-byes as we transferred to different buses.

My grandson now sitting next to me said, "Grandma, you talked with that woman all the way from New York to Albany. What were you talking about?"

"We were talking about the Word of God and Ruth gave her heart to Jesus." He understood what took place because he had given his heart to the Lord at a very young age. David never forgot what happened on that trip.

Many years later as David was ministering in song at a gospel music concert, he mentioned this bus ride and said, "My Grandmother talks to everyone about God. She doesn't hold back when it comes to witnessing. This is what each one of us should do, share God and our testimony with those who don't know the Lord."

This witnessing incident made a lasting impression on my ten-year old grandson. Even until today David, a worship leader and songwriter, is married with two sons and actively witnesses to souls about the Lord.

I finally arrived at home after nine hours on the bus. Tired as I was from the trip, early the next day I went to the bookstore to buy a special Bible with a concordance. The owner knew we had many Bibles in our church and was curious to know why I wanted this special Bible. I told him about the bus trip witnessing experience. When I finished telling him about the young woman who accepted the Lord, he said to me, "There will be no charge for this Bible. We want to be a part of this conversion by giving her the Word of Life as a gift. A simple bus trip brought salvation to another soul, praise God!

A Union President Receives Christ

While I was teaching at a High School in Buffalo, our union decided to go on strike. A meeting was held with hundreds of teachers present to discuss a possible settlement. I did not want to go alone, so I asked Mrs. Moore, my prayer partner, to come with me.

We arrived at the meeting and sat towards the back of the auditorium. We listened to the speakers and stayed until the meeting was over.

Our union president came on stage and then shared with us that he was being falsely accused of some wrongdoing and would most likely be sent to prison for a short time. Hearing this, something inside of me said, "Have compassion. Go up and pray with him." Wow, that was a big order to fulfill! I knew it had to be the Lord speaking because I only knew him by name.

I shared this with Mrs. Moore and she said, "If that is what God wants you to do, I will come with you."

My first thought was, "What will some of the teachers and principals think if they see me go backstage? 'What is Mrs. Franco doing going up there?' " My mind wasted no time telling me that I would make a fool of myself if I went backstage. However, in spite of the possibility of being embarrassed, I still had an overriding holy boldness come over me.

The meeting was almost finished when the president made his way backstage. "I think we should go now," said Mrs. Moore. We quietly walked down the outer aisle and up the side stairway leading to the backstage area.

There in a far off corner was the president. He first looked over at us as if to say, "What are you women doing here?"

Immediately, I introduced Mrs. Moore and myself to him and said, "We want you to know how badly we feel about the news. We would like to pray that God will be with you, if you agree."

"I thank you for your concern, and I would gladly appreciate your prayer."

"Jesus will be with you even in your prison cell if you believe that Jesus is the Son of God and accept Him into your heart as Lord and Savior of your life." I can't put in words the awesome presence of God that was felt in that room. I saw a beam of light surrounding the three of us. It seemed as though we were the only ones in the room.

The president, touched by the Holy Spirit, willingly repeated a simple Sinner's Prayer. We prayed a prayer of thanksgiving, comfort and protection over him during this testing period in his life. Then the Lord gave me a Word of Knowledge for him that he would not be alone for God would be with him, honor him, and set him free. We ended our conversation by letting him know that we would keep him in our prayers.

Can God be in the midst a secular meeting with hundreds of teachers and save a union president? "For where two or three are gathered in my name there I am in the midst of them" (Matthew 18:20). God converts the sinner, but he needs us as his ambassadors to deliver the message of salvation.

The Best Christmas Gift Ever

While working at a Real Estate office, I learned that it was their tradition to exchange gifts at Christmas time. I am a firm believer of buying gifts that are useful and lasting. I did a little praying and mind searching, and it seemed that whatever my mind suggested just did not seem to be useful.

One morning as I woke up, an unusual gift idea came before me. As I thought upon this gift, the flesh, which is always at enmity with the spirit, began to put second thoughts in my mind. "Now if you give that gift, what will they think of you? They will all be giving everyday earthly gifts, and here you come along with Bibles and a CD with Christian songs. They will probably laugh at your gifts. Just go along with them and buy a personal coffee mug or something like that!"

Wow, what a battle! But then I thought, "Well what better gift can I give to the boss, his wife, and the other agents than the living Word of God. I will write a personal message in each Bible with life-giving scriptures and wrap them in beautiful Christmas wrapping paper. That's it, my decision is made." Once I overcame the negative thoughts, I knew this the best gift that I could give as a witness for my stand and belief in God. There was only one other born-again Christian coworker in our office. The others were all unsaved.

The time came to exchange gifts. I wish I had had a video camera to take pictures of the expressions of surprise on all of their faces. They each told me, "What a wonderful gift." I never could have dreamed what was about to happen. By giving them the best gift ever, the Holy Bible and the Christian songs, I opened up a door for witnessing.

Debbie, the office manager, said, "Rose, while growing up in my parent's home, we were not allowed to have a Bible or to read one. Until today, I have never opened a Bible." Weeks later she approached me and said, "Rose every night I read the Bible with my husband." Another woman asked me to teach her how to use the

Bible. She said, "Rose I want what you have. Please tell me what I need to do." I shared the message of salvation, she accepted the Lord as her Savior. The broker and his wife took the Bible home and began comparing it with their Catholic Bible. With God's help, I answered their many questions.

One Saturday morning Debbie and I were the only ones in the office when the phone rang. It was our broker's wife. She related the sad news that her husband, who was in his late 40s, had been rushed to the hospital. He had suffered a sudden heart attack while celebrating a weekend with his wife. Doctors gave little hope for his recovery. Debbie, began crying, "Rose, what are we going to do now?" I told her that the best thing we could do was to pray for him.

"Before we can pray together, I must ask you if you have ever accepted Jesus as the Son of God and invited Him into her heart? What has happened to the broker can happen to anyone of us; therefore it's important that we are ready for heaven."

"Rose, I have never heard these things before. Yes, I want Jesus to come into my heart because I want to be ready." As we prayed together Debbie accepted the Lord into her heart. Then we prayed for our broker, asking God to save his soul and heal his body. Our broker was a former member of the Hell's Angels.

While he was in the hospital, I sent him a card with the message of salvation and told him, "Remember that each added day in your life has been given to you by God because He loves you."

While the broker was still in the hospital and feeling better, he sent each one of us flowers with a personal note attached. My note read, "To God's child." That was my answer. Beyond the entire hard surface and whatever possessed him, he recognized God in my life. I believe God was working on him for quite some time. When he returned to the office, I told him again that God had healed him and extended his life. At that time, he refused to give God any credit. But God kept dealing with him.

A few months later, after I had left that real estate company, I received a phone call from the broker's wife saying, "Rose are you standing or sitting? You will not believe what happened to my husband. We started attending a Full Gospel Christian Church. He received Christ into his heart, and now he wants to be water baptized. Rose, my husband is a changed man. Every night we read the Bible you have given us. I had to call and let you know this because you and your life had a part in us receiving Christ. For my husband to give his heart to the Lord, it had to be a miracle!"

How affective was this gift, the Holy Bible? Four lives received life eternal, and only God knows how many more lives have come to know the Lord through their testimony. I dare you to give the Bible as an exchange gift at your place of employment and let the Lord do the rest.

A Timely Word

When we were holding a week of special services in Merritt Island, each night the pastor of the church had me share a few words of greetings before my husband delivered the sermon.

Our last service at the church was on Sunday morning. We were staying at the parsonage next door to the church. My husband had left for the service an hour earlier and I had planned to join him later. Before leaving he said, "Rose, because we need time the travel to another church this evening service, I will go right into the sermon without you sharing, okay?"

"John, that's fine, I understand."

I was in the bathroom getting ready when I noticed a basket full of Christian Literature. Among them, was a copy of the *Evangel* magazine. The title of an article, "From Formalism to Fanaticism," caught my attention. I could not help but read the article.

I heard a voice say, *"Now relate this to your field of art."* As I thought upon these words, it was as though a light bulb went on in my head. I thought, "How true, the spiritual experience is like the field of art in one sense. On the art spectrum there are many different types of art. Three types of art seemed to come before me as I continued to read. They were mechanical drawing, realism and abstract. Likewise in the religious world there are many different beliefs and modes of worship. I focused in on three types of Christian worship:

Formalism: The Word of God as form or law

Humanism: The Word in Part as a person understands it

Charismatic: Believing in the Fullness and the Power of the Word with the manifestations of the Holy Spirit.

Formalistic churches use a set format for their services. It does not allow any room for the Holy Spirit to move. This we call the Word spoken as form or law. 2 Timothy 3:5 states "Having a form of godliness, but denying the power thereof: from such turn away."

The same applies to mechanical drawing in the field of art. It is found at the far left of the spectrum. Mechanical drawing has a set of plans to go by and one does not deviate from these plans whatsoever. Therefore there is no room for creativity.

Let us go to the middle of the art spectrum. Here we find realism where no two people can see a scene or an object in the same way. I once gave a test to 200 women at a weekend retreat. They were to render a drawing of the art composition consisting of a single object, which was a vase. We checked the results and we were unable to find two drawings alike. This test proves that everyone has his or her own visual perception. Therefore, we all think and see things differently.

Isn't this also true in the spiritual realm? In the middle of the spiritual spectrum, we find Humanism: Christians who believe the Word in part. They see through their human eyes. They choose to believe the Word in part according to their own understanding. They cannot experience the fullness of God's revelation in their lives. They know the Word of God, love the Lord and are spiritually satisfied by living in the comfort zone. Their spiritual eyes are not fully opened to receive the greater promises of God that can only be envisioned when the Holy Spirit has full preeminence in their lives.

To the far right of the art spectrum, we find abstract art. People will look at an abstract painting and say, "What is that?" This question arises because the viewer cannot understand the hidden deeper searching and sensitivity the artist experiences. The artist himself knew what he was doing. He had an idea and he brought it out on canvas using space, colors, shades, hues, shapes and balance in creating a work of art.

Let us look to the far right of the spiritual spectrum called Charismatic worship. We see what some people might call fanaticism because they don't understand the moving of the Holy Spirit. The Charismatic Christian places God as the source of all things. God is in control. This spiritual realm is where Christians believe in the fullness of the Holy Spirit, its power and the sovereignty of God. Putting aside their natural eyes and seeing fully through their spiritual eyes, they understand and receive the spiritual promises. To experience the manifestation of the Holy Spirit and its ministries, we must go beyond the comfort zone of Humanism and enter into the Charismatic zone of faith and freedom.

We will never fully understand the workings and miracles of God, for they go beyond human understanding and limitation. Therefore, we must dare to believe God through faith for things we cannot understand with our human mind or see with our natural eyes. Hebrews 11:1 states "Now faith is the substance of things hoped for, the evidence of things not seen."

With these spiritual applications in mind, I wrote down some notes and placed them in my purse. When I looked up at the clock, I realized that the service was going to start in ten minutes. So I quickly finished dressing and hurried across the parking lot to attend the meeting.

During the service the pastor stood up and thanked my husband and me for ministering to the congregation. Then he said, "Before Reverend Franco speaks this morning, how many of you would like to hear Mrs. Franco share a few words with us?" They applauded with a big "Amen!" I was ready to graciously refuse his request because of the time constraints. But I heard an inner voice say, *"Tell them about the article you just read. They need to hear it."* Knowing it was the Holy Spirit speaking, I obeyed. I looked at my husband. He motioned with his eyes that he was in agreement.

I stepped up to the pulpit and began to share the article I had read, "From Formalism to Fanaticism." I related the spiritual application of the article and compared it to the field of art from mechanical drawing to abstract. I tried to simplify it as much as possible in a short time. I recall emphasizing, "God loves you and wants to reveal Himself to you. As you lean not on your own understanding, but by faith open your spiritual eyes, then and only then can you experience all that God has for you." With this I quietly went back to my seat.

Little did I know that a husband, wife and three children were in the service for the first time. They were driving by and saw the sign in front of the church, announcing the special meetings. They were not churchgoers. The wife asked her husband, "Why don't we stop and see what these meetings are all about."

At the close of my husband's sermon, as usual, he gave an invitation for Salvation. This family went up to the altar to receive Christ as their personal Savior.

Then the husband and wife greeted me, introduced themselves as Mr. & Mrs. Adams and thanked me for sharing the Word. Mrs. Adams went on to say, "While you were speaking, I felt two hands embracing me from the back. I turned around and no one was there, but I believe it was God letting me know that He is real and that He loved me. And I must tell you that I am a freelance artist. The way you explained the spiritual aspect of life and related it to my field of art made something happen inside of me. For the first time my eyes were opened to understand the spiritual things of God. Now it all makes sense to me." Her face was glowing with the presence of the Lord.

One year later we were holding meetings at the same church. As we entered the church, the pastor's wife approached me saying, "Do you remember that couple sitting there in the pew?" I hesitated for a moment trying to recall and before I could answer, she said, "They are Mr. & Mrs. Adams, the couple who accepted the Lord when you were here last year. I can't tell you enough about them. They are faithfully attending all the church services. Mrs. Adams is assisting in the children's church, and her husband is an usher." They have been a tremendous blessing to us. When we greeted them, they were anxious to tell us how their lives were changed since they walked into the church on that Sunday morning.

A timely word directed by the Holy Spirit, will bring results. The Lord knew that a freelance artist and her family would be in the service that morning. The Holy Spirit inspired me to read the article and relate it to my field of art. An opportunity arose for me to share what God had given me. God had preordained all this as part of His plan for the salvation of this family of five.

God's plan is like a puzzle to us. We know that all the pieces must be in place in order to complete the full picture. I will say it again, *"Who can fathom the greatness of God? Who can fully understand the way He works His wonders to perform?"* We only know in part the great mysteries of God. 1 Corinthians 13:12 states

"For now we see through a glass, darkly; but then face to face: now I know in part; but then shall I know even as also I am known."

There are times when God will use us as ambassadors to bring about His will and purpose. It is very important that we are in tune with His Spirit. We must recognize His voice, follow His leading and have the courage to speak a timely word inspired by the Holy Spirit.

Only heaven knows how many souls have been won because someone, somewhere, had the courage to speak a timely word given by the inspiration of the Holy Spirit.

Our prayer should be as the songwriter penned:

"Lord, I'll be a witness, If you will help my weakness,

For surely there's a work that I can do, And even though it's humble, do cause my will to crumble,

And though the task be great, I'll work for thee."

There is nothing in this world that can give you the joy that comes from witnessing and leading a soul to the Lord.

Chapter Six

MIRACLES OF PROTECTION

———

Forever Grateful

When we look back at some of the incidents that transpired in our lives, we become more aware of how many times God has divinely brought protection and deliverance from tragic situations. I think back to when my son Bob was in fifth grade. The class went on a field trip to the Long Island Sound. About six feet from the shore, the water depth increases suddenly to about 12 feet high. If one is not familiar with this drop, it can be very dangerous or even fatal especially for young children.

I did want to accompany my son on the field trip, but I was working full time and five months pregnant. At first I thought, "Maybe I shouldn't let him go without me." But knowing how he was looking forward to this school outing, I gave in and let him go. He knew I was concerned and said, "Mom, don't worry. I promise you I'll be careful." I got Bob off to school, and I went to work at the office.

While at work, I suddenly sensed an urgency to go and be with my son. At first I thought, "This must be my imagination." Since I was always very protective of my children, this thought was quite normal for me. But a voice kept repeating in my mind, *"Go be with your son."*

I knew that Bob had had swimming lessons and was quite a good swimmer. Then I heard those words again. But this time in a louder, more compelling voice, *"Hurry. Go to your son."* At this point, I knew without a doubt that the Lord was speaking to me for a reason.

I left work immediately and traveled about 25 minutes to the Sound. I found a parking space and quickly went down to the beach area. As a concerned mother, I first looked for my son. As I spotted him in the water, I noticed that he was going down, and then he came up and started to go down again.

My son was drowning. There were no lifeguards at the beach, and as a swimmer, I knew what that meant. I ran toward the water and let out a scream as loud as I could, *"Please help my son. He is drowning!"* I pointed to my son and then I dove into the water in spite of my condition. I couldn't swim very fast due to my pregnancy.

But I noticed that a father and his daughter heard me yell for help. They were in the water swimming in another direction, but they changed their course and began swimming toward my son. They grabbed him from the water and began swimming back to shore with him. When they were closer to the shore, I grabbed my son's foot. I didn't want to lose him.

Really, I didn't save my son. It was the Lord who spoke to my heart to go. He had me arrive just in time. A few minutes later my son would had drowned. I knew God was watching over him. The Lord had the father and daughter team swimming in the water at that exact time when my son was going down for the third time. *"I am forever grateful to you, Lord, for saving my son's life and thank you Holy Spirit for the warning."*

Angels in Disguise

A most unusual experience happened during one train ride to the Business School in Jamaica, Long Island. Every morning before my mother drove me to the train station, she prayed for God's protection upon her daughter. I traveled by train for 1½ hours with two other girls from my hometown. During that time I worked on my homework.

About an hour into our train ride, the girls decided that they would skip school and go to a movie in New York City. They were begging me to go with them. I always had a fear of doing something displeasing to God and to my mother. I knew it would be wrong for me to go with them. I had never done anything like that before.

They did not stop, repeatedly insisting that I go with them. I told them, "I'm not allowed to come with you."

They said, "Oh, don't worry, your mother will never know. We will be home in time for her to meet you at the station."

Again I said, "No, I'm sorry, but I will not come with you."

While this was happening, I heard someone singing. It was coming from the seats to the left of us. As I listened carefully I heard a song that was very familiar to me. It was a song that we sang at our church, *"Yield not to temptation, for yielding is sin."* As I looked in the direction of where this warning was coming from, I saw two Rabbis pointing their fingers at me. They repeated the song again. A fear and sense of guilt gripped my heart. I thought to myself, *"God must be watching over me to allow these men to sing this warning song to me."*

As we approached the stop for my school, the Rabbis continued to sing warning me not to go, but the girls were telling me not to listen. As I hesitated, the train left the station and I had not gotten off. Even today I can never forget the look on the faces of the Rabbis, letting me know that I shouldn't have given in to the girls.

My God-fearing conscience was at work. It had already convicted me. I heard a voice within me say, *"Don't go with them. Get off at the next stop and go back to school."* I did not say anything to the girls, but as soon as the train stopped again I looked over at the Rabbis who nodded their heads, as if to say, *"Well done, my child."* And they gave me a big smile of approval. I got out just in time and made it back to school before my first class started.

God purposed for the two Rabbis to sit across from us. *Were they Rabbis or angels in disguise?* He used them to minister to me through the song, "Yield not to temptation, for yielding is sin." Not knowing much about Rabbis' worship songs, I was amazed to hear them sing one of the same songs we sang in our church. Mother's prayer for her daughter's protection was answered. He sent angels in the form of men, the two Rabbis. Psalms 91:11 tells us, "For He shall give His angles charge over thee, to keep thee in all thy ways." Is He not a God of originality, of creativity? Who can compare with His wisdom? We can say with all confidence, we serve a great God!

Obeying the Holy Spirit

I was debating whether or not I should write about an incident that occurred while I was teaching because of the intense message within its contents. But after sharing how God protected me with Krista my granddaughter who is a schoolteacher, she said, "Grandma, you must include this incident in your book. It's good for people to know what the Lord can do in a situation like this." I still pondered over the idea. Then the more I thought about it, the more I realized that someone may be enlighten and encouraged to be open to the warning of the Holy Spirit in a similar situation.

So, I cannot conclude this chapter without sharing and giving God the glory for protecting me from a near death situation. It happened when I was teaching at a high school. To better grasp the full understanding of why an incident of this nature could happen, I first have to paint a picture of the whole teaching situation.

I was teaching five different art subjects at an inner city high school. My students were excelling in art. Some were doing very outstanding work. I had entered my students in an art show with 32 other high schools. It was the first time our school was represented in an art show.

The Department of Art Education at Albany, New York highly commended my students' artwork. They later sent me a letter complimenting my students for doing the most outstanding artwork from among all the other schools represented. My students were doing live portrait drawings of shoppers, using charcoal media. Some of students were engaged in other types of artwork. One particular student named Adam drew a lot of attention. In fact, one of our district administrators purchased one of his works of art.

Not long after this I was called into the head principal's office. This was my first time in his office. Whenever there was a problem, we conferred with the assistant principal. With the approval of the Baptist assistant principal, we had started a Bible club. I was concerned about the Bibles I kept in my desk. But I found out soon enough that the Bibles were not the reason why Dr. Smith had asked to see me.

The time for my appointment with the principal came. He immediately directed my attention to a file in his office and said, "Mrs. Franco, do you avail yourself of these student files?"

My answer was, "No, Dr. Smith, is this a requirement?"

He answered, "No, but most teachers use these files to check the backgrounds on students' previous behavioral problems. For instance, see this file on Adam. Look at his past school history. He has always had problems. Now for the first time, Adam made the honor roll. His teachers tell me he gets all his work done so he can come to your classroom. They want to know what you are doing to motivate him."

My response to his inquiry was, "Dr. Smith, I believe that I am making lasting imprints on my students that will affect them for the rest of their lives, either for good or for bad. I trust for good. I think of them as individuals who have diversified talents. My goal is to recognize their abilities and encourage confidence needed to excel in art and in every area of their lives."

Dr. Smith looked at me and gave me a little smile of approval and said, "Whatever you are doing must be helping."

There were so many good things happening for my students, body, mind and spirit, and Satan did not like it. Among my students I had a drug pusher and a Satanist student. These two students did very good artwork in my drawing classes. Some of their artwork was hanging in our school art gallery.

In spite of a security guard in the hall right outside my classroom once a week drugs were being exchanged in my room. I knew how dangerous it would be for me to say anything. The best thing was to mind my own business, say nothing and keep my focus on teaching. If the security guards knew what was going on and were not stopping it, I would be foolish to get involved. Who would believe me? I didn't know how long I could take this, knowing in my heart what was happening. It seemed that God put me there for more than just teaching art.

My art supervisor in the district did not want me teaching there. He had wanted to put me with advanced students because of my background of achievements in the field of art. Believe me, this was a rough school. Friends and other teachers would say to me, "How can you teach there? It's one the worse schools." I was told about some frightening incidents that happened to some of the previous teachers.

I said to the Lord, *"What am I doing here? It is so dangerous. I know we started a Bible club, something that was never approved before and students are getting saved. But Lord, the drug traffic in this school is just too much. I don't know how much longer I can endure this. Please protect me and keep me safe."*

There was such a love from all of my students, except from the drug pusher and the Satanist student. I could sense their attitudes, but I treated them the same as the other students.

What I had been sensing began to openly manifest itself when the Satanist student came up to me in the classroom one day before the other students arrived. He brought in a painting he had done at home. It was a painting of Satan with written words that said, "If you harken unto me I will give you all the riches of this world." Then all around this image of Satan were oval shaped paintings of human figures doing evil practices of darkness.

This boy looked straight into my eyes and said, "I want this to be displayed downstairs in the art gallery." As soon as I first saw the painting, my nonverbal utterance was *God, cover me with the blood of Jesus, protect me and give me the wisdom I need to handle his request.* It was at this point that I realized he was a Satanist.

I looked at him and said, "You have a message in this painting, and we are not allowed to solicit or display any written material."

Again with staring eyes he repeated, "This painting must be displayed."

I immediately responded, "I will go to the assistant principal and show it to him and let him decide." I said this to quiet the student, knowing the principal would not approve.

I went directly to the assistant principal with the painting and explained the conversation I had with the student. When he saw the painting, he was in shock with disbelief just as I was. "Rose, you tell that student to come to my office." I went back and conveyed the message to him, and needless to say, he was very distraught. In class he kept to himself except for talking with the drug pusher who sat next to him. I noticed that they had become close friends.

About a month later while in my classroom, I received an unexpected phone call from the assistant principal. He said, "I know you are not aware, but we are going to have a drug bust in your room at 10 a.m. Don't be alarmed and don't say anything." Wow, was I frightened; yet I had to be composed. I had no idea what this all would involve or what would happen. I never spoke to anyone about the drug trafficking. I did not know if this was a routine procedure or if the word got around about the drug traffic through students.

The drug bust occurred at ten o'clock. We were all frightened. We were all told to leave while the policemen searched the room. I was never told if any drugs were found. After the drug bust took place the drug trafficking subsided. Everything seemed to go back to normal. But little did I know what was being planned for me by the drug pusher and the Satanist.

A few weeks later during my free period, I was preparing my art materials for the last class of the day. I heard a voice, the Holy Spirit, say *"Don't move away from your desk during the next class."* I made very little of it and continued to work at my desk. Then twice more I heard the same message. Each time it was louder and louder. After the third time, I was sure the Holy Spirit was speaking to me. A strong sense of obedience arose within me.

As I obeyed the leading of the Holy Spirit, a surge of strength sprang up within me. I felt the shield of faith around me, like one going to battle. Little did I know the spiritual battle that would take place, but my Lord knew, and He prepared me for the battle. I said to the Lord, *"I know you are with me; I pray for your divine protection. Put your consuming wall of fire around me as I follow your leading."*

I looked to see how far the telephone was from my desk, in the event I needed to call for help. I also left my classroom door open for an easy exit, if needed. After heeding to the Holy Spirit's warning I knew I had to take precautions. I could hear, *"Be alert and stand firm."*

The students all came in the classroom, very sober and extremely quiet with their heads down. This already was unusual. As they were all seated, I took the attendance and only one student was missing from class. The drug pusher and the Satan worshipper were in the last row to the right of me. The Holy Spirit focused my attention in their direction. As I looked, I noticed they were busy talking to each other. Rather then sitting at their desk as usual, they were both standing.

I sensed in my spirit at that point that they were up to no good. My classroom was located on the third floor. These two students sat next to a large window. We had been given orders by the school administration not to open the windows because the window pulleys were damaged and a window could fall down unexpectedly and cause injuries to someone. Therefore, the windows were never opened. But these students, after talking to each other, went over to that window and opened it. I was suspicious of their motive, even though I did not know this was part of their plan. I must say that this account is hard for me to recollect because of the intensity of the incident, but I must continue, so I can give God the glory for what He has done.

After observing the behavior of these students, I had a witness in my spirit that this was going to be a spiritual battle. By nature I am not a loud or boisterous person, but on that day I believe the Lord gave me boldness and courage to speak with authority. I told all the students, "I will not be walking around the classroom today. If you need help you must come up to my desk." I was following the leading of the Holy Spirit.

The minute I said this, about ten students, some of them big football players, all stood to their feet and surrounded my desk. They seemed to have an expression of relief upon their faces. You would think that the normal thing to do would be for each student to come up individually.

The Holy Spirit got my attention again concerning the students who surrounded my desk, *"These are your protecting angels in disguise."* As these students were exchanging in conversation with me, the drug pusher began calling out to me with a heavy demanding voice, "Mrs. Franco, come back here!"

At first I did not answer, but as he kept repeating this I firmly said, "I will not be partial. If you need help you must come to my desk." While all this was taking place, the ten students never moved away from my desk. I believe that they were faithfully guarding the post that God ordained for my protection.

The pieces of the puzzle were all falling in place: the opening of the window, trying to get me to go to them, and the ten angels that were protecting me. I received the picture loud and clear. Between speaking with my ten students, I silently was calling on the blood of Jesus, rebuking the power of darkness. It seemed that the more I pleaded the blood of Jesus, the angrier they became, calling out to me. By this time, I kept reminding myself about the phone and the open door. The second thought was to dismiss my students early and leave with them.

I began ignoring their demands and stopped responding to their outburst. Again they were talking to each other, and planning another strategy. As I looked in their direction, without making it obvious to them, I noticed expressions of anger on their faces. Finally, realizing that their previous plans were not working, they said to me, "If you do not come to us, we will come and get you." What an unbelievable nightmare this was for me. My angels were not afraid. They were still surrounding me!

The devil was losing ground. Little did they know who was on my side fighting the battle. There was no more time to lose. I could not use the phone because they would have stopped me. I had to follow the second thought of dismissing the class about 20 minutes earlier, something I'd never done before. As soon as I announced this, the ten students and all the others, aside from those two students, stayed close to me as we left and even walked me to my car. Not one student said a word about what had happened.

When I walked into my house, I was still shaking about what took place. I told my husband, "John, a terrible thing happened today. I feel my life is in danger. I might have to leave this school." I shared with him what the Lord told me to do. He tried to comfort me and ease my concern. But the concern lingered on my mind. From the warning given me by the Holy Spirit it was obvious that something was planned to hurt or take my life.

The next day during my lunch period, I locked my room, something I had never done before. About ten minutes later I heard a knock at my door. I reluctantly looked through the window section of the door and to my amazement I saw James, the student who had missed class the day before. As I opened the door I could see him looking up and down the hall to see if anyone was watching him. I wasn't surprised. He had good reason to feel that way.

I let him in the room and locked the door again. He nervously said, "Please, Mrs. Franco, let's move away from the door. I am so happy to see you here. I didn't want to see anything bad happen to you. That is why I missed class."

With this I said, "James, where did you expect me to be?"

Then James replied, "Please don't tell anyone, but they had planned to hurt you by pushing you out the window because the drug pusher thought you called for a drug bust on him. The other boy was against you for not displaying his painting. They told us if we said anything about this to you, they would kill our mothers."

I told him, "James, what if I tell you I knew all about this before it happened?"

James responded, "Who told you, Mrs. Franco?"

"The Lord told me not to move from my desk and sent His angels around me."

"He did Mrs. Franco?"

"Yes James, God protected me."

"I am so happy you are here because we all like you."

After confirming the warning that the Holy Spirit had given me, I decided as long as the drug pusher was in my class, it was time for me to give up my job at that school. That same evening I told my husband about the confirmation and my decision. I had planned to see my art supervisor about my decision on Monday morning. I could no longer ignore the writing on the wall.

During supper we were watching the evening news on television. They were reporting on a bank robbery. I recognized the third person in the robbery as the drug pusher from my class. They said he was shot in the head and that his wound was critical. I couldn't believe what I was seeing. My husband and I were speechless. The boy did not return to school for the rest of the semester.

After this happened, we decided that I would try to finish out the school year. It continued without any more incidents until the last full day of school. We had a light schedule that day. During the last period, Matthew, a student who had been in my class the previous year, was home from college and came to visit me. I was very glad to see him. He shared a little about his schooling.

Within about 15 minutes, to my shocking surprise, the drug pusher appeared in my classroom. Knowing about his critical injuries, I couldn't believe it was him. I thought I was seeing a ghost. I noticed all my students were afraid and appeared surprised. I'll never forget it. He was wearing a black trench coat with a black hat. He went to the back of the classroom. I was in a frozen state of mind, but I tried to compose myself. I said to myself, *"Lord, what is he doing here? After you spared my life, how come he is back here again on the last day of school?"*

As I acknowledged him, he began telling me that he had been accepted into an art school. Of course I complimented him. All this time, I was at my desk and Matthew was standing next to me. For some reason, I felt that he was protecting me. I had noticed that all the time the drug pusher was speaking, he kept his right hand in his pocket. Truthfully, the thought came to me, "He probably has a gun in his pocket." I thought, *"Oh, Lord you watched over me in the past. Please cover me with your blood and protect me against this evil."* Well, he did leave the class without any incident, thank God.

Unbeknown to me, God had another angel in disguise protecting me. How did I know? Many years later at one of my husband's special services, a man came up to us after the meeting and told us he was from Buffalo. In the course of the conversation, he asked me where I had taught. I told him the name of the high school. He remarked how bad the conditions were at that school.

When he realized what my name was, he told me he had known about the incident that happened to me at that school. He went on to say, *"It wasn't by chance that Matthew came to your classroom. He purposed to be there that day to protect you. Matthew had heard through the grapevine that the drug pusher was coming to your classroom with a gun and had intended to harm you. Matthew had a gun on him ready to shoot first if the drug pusher dared to show the very first sign of firing his gun at you."* For his protection, I cannot reveal how this man knew about this incident but this man said, *"God sent Matthew to you that day."*

I told him, "*I believe that God did send Matthew as another angel in disguise to protect me.*" I know my life was spared because I obeyed the Holy Spirit when He spoke to me three times telling me, "*Don't move away from your desk.*"

I could write a complete book just recounting the countless times that God has watched over my family and me. He may give us a warning through the Holy Spirit, or sometimes He commissions real angels, or uses them in disguise to protect us.

When in trouble call upon the Lord and He will protect and deliver you no matter what the situation may be. He fights the battle for us.

"He shall call upon me, and I will answer him: I will be with him in trouble; I will deliver him, and honour him." (Psalms 91:15). The angel of the Lord encampeth round about them that fear him, and delivereth them." (Psalms 34:7).

Chapter Seven

REVELATION BY VISIONS AND DREAMS

———

Dreams and Visions

My first experience with God began at an early age. I clearly remember walking barefooted across the soft cool green grass, observing the beautiful trees with leaves of many colors and shapes. Then I glanced at the clear blue sky with uniquely shaped white cotton-like clouds floating in space; I looked in amazement at the beauty of God's creation. I began to develop an awareness of God's presence. I knew from my Sunday school teachings that God created the heavens and the earth but that day the greatness of God became a reality to me. I remember looking up to heaven and telling Jesus how much I loved Him. It was on that day that my journey with the Lord began.

A short time after this experience, the Lord began to show me visions. In the visions Jesus would appear to me and give me a message. I shared my first vision with my mother.

As I was bubbling over with joy, I told her, "Mamma, I saw Jesus when I was praying and He talked to me!"

"What did Jesus tell you, Rosina?"

As I told her about my vision, she was amazed that God would give a vision to a child. But knowing that the Bible spoke about the young seeing visions, she accepted it as a message from the Lord. Several of these visions followed and some were answers to prayers.

Then at the age of ten, the Lord appeared to me in a vision with a sad expression on His face. He said, "My child, I will not come to you in this way any longer, for you have reached an age of understanding where men will not believe you." I began to cry. At that time, I did not understand the meaning of what He said. I wondered if Jesus didn't love me anymore. My mother reassured me that He did indeed still loves me. As I grew older, I began to understand the meaning of the last vision.

Several years later, my mother shared with me some of the miracles that God brought about through these visions. A woman had lost a considerable amount of weight due to a severe stomach ailment. Her food intake was at a minimum. In the vision the Lord had told me her name and said, "Tell her to eat everything in my name and no harm will come to her." When my mother gave her the message, she accepted it as a word from the Lord. By faith she followed the instructions and was totally healed. God spoke to a child in a vision. The messenger delivered the word. It was accepted by faith and a miracle was birth.

Later on in life, I experienced other types of visions, not like those that I had experienced as a child. In my walk with the Lord, there were times when I went to God for guidance and direction. Sometimes He used visual images through visions or dreams to reveal a need or an answer to a prayer.

An answer to a prayer came about through a dream of reassurance and guidance. It dealt with our first full-time pastoral assignment.

We had been living within two blocks of all our relatives before the move. I knew it would be a great adjustment for our children to be uprooted from their safe and comfortable environment. The assignment was located in Youngstown, Ohio, about 12 hours away from our loved ones.

As I shared in a previous chapter, due to my son's illness I was unable to accompany my husband when he went to candidate. While my husband was away, I prayed according to the Word of God, "In all thy ways acknowledge him, and he shall direct thy paths." Proverbs 3:6. I wanted to know the will of God for our lives and ministry. I asked Him, "If this is the church where you want us to go, please Lord give me a sign or a word."

That night while I was sleeping, the Lord gave me a dream that I was in Youngstown, Ohio. In the dream, I was cleaning the springs under the mattresses. As I was doing this, I turned to my husband and said, "John, I must let our families know our new address." I stopped cleaning and grabbed a sheet of paper and began writing, "Landsdown Blvd., Youngstown, Ohio." I had never been in Youngstown, so this address meant nothing to me.

When my husband returned from Ohio, I shared with him that I had had a dream that I was living on Landsdown Blvd. With an expression of surprise he looked at me. Then, before I could finish telling him my dream, he politely interrupted me and said, "Rose, that is the address of the church parsonage!"

I was speechless for a moment, thinking, "God, your word never fails. Thank you for directing our path and confirming your word." After that revelation, we both knew that Youngstown was where God wanted us to go and minister.

I recall another dream where God revealed someone's need. We had stopped overnight at a hotel on our way to hold a series of meetings. That night the Lord gave me a dream about a minister's wife from one of the churches where we would be ministering. The details of the dream were very personal. The dream would not leave me. I said to the Lord, "I cannot approach that woman and tell her this. If you want me to pray with her, please Lord, let her open up to me."

At the church, I was scheduled to speak at the women's fellowship meeting. A wonderful presence of the Holy Spirit was evident during the prayer time. Immediately after prayer, we were invited downstairs for fellowship and refreshments.

While at the beverage table, getting myself a hot drink, the pastor's wife called me into another room. She was crying as she began sharing some deep issues that were going on in her life. At the beginning of our conversation, I shared with her that in a dream God had burdened me to pray for her. Weeping, she held my hand and asked me to pray for her and her family. As we prayed, she broke down and confessed what was on her heart. The presence of the Lord was in that room. Deliverance and healing came, a family was restored, and a ministry was saved.

There are additional dreams and visions recorded in some of the other chapters that God had revealed to bring about His will and purpose in a particular situation.

Many lives have been spared from hardships or even death through a warning revealed by the Lord in a dream. Others have received direction or comfort for their lives. Today, even as in the days of old, God still reveals Himself to His people through dreams and visions. God has not changed. The God of yesterday is the God of today.

Throughout the Bible from Genesis to Revelation God spoke to prophets, disciples and people through dreams and visions. The dreams and visions were divine revelations from God revealing prophetic messages of things present and things to come. Other messages were warnings, guidance or encouragement. The following scriptures confirm that dreams and visions are for today.

In Genesis 46:2-3 God spoke to Jacob in a vision. "And God spake unto Israel in the visions of the night, and said, Jacob, Jacob. And he said, Here am I. And he said, I am God, the God of thy father: fear not to go down into Egypt; for I will there make of thee a great nation:"

The prophet Joel, in the Old Testament, Joel 2:28, foretold what would happen in the days ahead. Then in the New Testament in Acts 2:17 Peter reminds the people of what was spoken of by the prophet Joel. "And it shall come to pass in the last days, saith God, I will pour out of my Spirit upon all flesh: and your sons and your daughters shall prophesy, and your young men shall see visions, and your old men shall dream dreams:"

Let's look at the dreams that are recorded in Matthew 2:12-13. "And being warned of God in a dream that they should not return to Herod, they departed into their own country another way. And when they were departed, behold, the angel of the Lord appeareth to Joseph in a dream, saying, Arise, and take the young child and his mother, and flee into Egypt, and be thou there until I bring thee word: for Herod will seek the young child to destroy him."

I can't imagine what would have happened to young Jesus if God did not warn Joseph in a dream to flee into Egypt. But Joseph obeyed God's warning, and so our Savior's life was spared to fulfill His mission on earth.

In Acts 16:9, God revealed to Paul through a vision where he should go and minister. "And a vision appeared to Paul in the night; There stood a man of Macedonia, and prayed him, saying, Come over into Macedonia, and help us."

We read in Acts 18:9-10, "Then spake the Lord to Paul in the night by a vision, Be not afraid, but speak, and hold not thy peace: For I am with thee, and no man shall set on thee to hurt thee: for I have much people in this city." God reassured Paul that He was with him and encouraged him to stay on and minister in Corinth.

These are only a few of the many scriptures in the Bible relating to dreams and visions.

Is God still revealing His will through dreams and visions today? Yes! Yesterday, today and until the end of time, God has and will communicate with us through dreams and visions.

Antique Canning Jars

While packing for a move from Buffalo, New York, to Arizona, my husband and I sorted through our belongings. Among them we found antique canning jars that had sentimental memories for me. My dear mother had used them for years. Mother's canning days were over. Knowing that we had a garden and canned most of our harvest, she had passed them on to us.

I treasured these canning jars. Each one was a constant reminder of mother's endless hours of love and hard labor. In spite of working to support five children, she always took time for her vegetable garden. The garden included fresh herbs. She would use these herbs in cooking the most delicious, healthy meals for us and for our friends.

My husband told me that we had to get rid of the canning jars. "John, you're breaking my heart. It's hard for me to part with these jars." I was reluctant, looking for a way to keep them. "Can't we ship them out by mail?"

He responded with, "No, glass jars are too fragile, they probably will break. Put them up for sale in the classified section of our weekly newspaper. Maybe someone will buy them."

I could barely hold back my tears as I sat down to write the ad. I tried hard to make the ad unattractive: "Canning Jars For Sale." As an obedient wife, I delivered the ad to the newspaper office. But, I must confess, I thought to myself, "In today's world, how many people are interested in canning?" This gave me some hope that somehow I would be able to keep my jars.

With this in mind, I went to the library and researched the age, type of glass and style of these jars. I discovered that some of them had great value, especially the blue-rippled designed ones. Many of the other jars also had significant value. I asked myself, "How could I give up these valuable canning jars?" Then I decided not to worry. I didn't think anyone would answer the ad.

But, sure enough, to my surprise, the very same day that the newspaper arrived on the newsstand, I received a call from a woman who was interested in purchasing all my canning jars. She gave us her address and phone number.

"How much are you asking for the jars?" she asked.

Without thinking, I said, "Fourteen dollars."

She replied, "Great! I'll take them all, but you will have to deliver them to my home."

What! Fourteen dollars for the three bushels of canning jars! She also wants them delivered to her home eight miles away! I was ready to tell her, "I changed my mind about selling my jars." Instead, something compelled me to say, "Tomorrow morning at 11 a.m. we will be at your home."

Was this really me speaking? I honestly didn't want to sell them. What made me agree to give them up so easily to the first caller? Within seconds, the Holy Spirit invaded my thoughts with a still small voice telling me not to worry, *"Your canning jars will still be your treasure. Wait and see."* Then suddenly without knowing how this could ever happen, I experienced feelings of joy and peace about releasing the canning jars.

My husband was unable to go with me. I was unfamiliar with that area of West Seneca. He told me, "Call Mrs. Moore, your prayer partner. Maybe she will go with you." Immediately, I called Mrs. Moore and shared with her the reason for my call.

Without hesitation, she said, "I'll be happy to go with you." I did breathe a sigh of relief, knowing I would not be alone. Going to a strange place, not knowing who or what I would encounter, was a little frightening. And who was better to be with me then my prayer partner!

That night after having my time in prayer, I retired for the evening. While I was sleeping, I had a dream that Mrs. Moore and I had gone to this woman's home. The woman came out of her home in a wheelchair. She looked at us and very softly said to us, "Look at my leg and thigh. I was in a car accident, and I was severely burned."

At that point I awoke from my dream. I thought, "What can this dream mean?" I went back to sleep, but when I awoke that morning the dream stayed with me.

I quickly went about my morning chores and then I looked at the clock; it was 10 a.m. I wanted to start early, just in case we had trouble finding this place. I put the canning jars in the car and drove to pick up Mrs. Moore. We started our unpredictable journey.

It was a beautiful clear sunny day as we drove to West Seneca. From the main road, we had to make a right onto a long, winding, deserted, dirt road. We approached the end of the road, where we had to make a left turn. The area was desolate with only one house in view. As we got closer to it, we saw a sign that read, "No Trespassing." Between the sign and the poor condition of the property, we had reason to be apprehensive. It reminded us of a scene in a scary movie.

I stopped the car and told Mrs. Moore the dream that I had the night before. She felt the need to pray before going to the woman's home. After praying, we both knew without a doubt that the Lord wanted to do something. Not knowing what we would be confronted with or what was about to happen, Mrs. Moore prayed again, "God, your will be done this day. Go before us, protect us, and may the Holy Spirit lead and guide our visit with this woman."

I started the car and drove to the woman's home that was about 500 feet from where we had stopped to pray. As we approached the driveway of her home, the first thing we noticed was a wooden ramp leading to the entrance. Mrs. Moore and I looked at each other as we thought about the dream. Then we both looked up toward heaven and prayed, "Lord you intervene here. We are trusting you to be with us."

I was ready to open my car door when we were greeted by two large fierce-looking Doberman pinchers growling with their mouths wide open. They began to jump up against my car window. I knew that I had to act quickly and roll up my partially opened window. I made it just before they had time to attack us. It was obvious that these dogs were trained to attack anyone entering the property. Wow! Another prayer went up for protection as fear gripped our souls. We had second thoughts about being there.

I immediately honked my horn repeatedly, hoping and praying that someone would come to the door. Finally, the door of the home opened, and a woman came out of the house, being pushed in a wheelchair by her husband down the ramp. The husband put the dogs in the house and came out to the car.

The woman's husband carried the bushels out of my car. They were so excited and pleased with the canning jars. They couldn't believe I had asked for only 14 dollars for so many antique canning jars. The transaction for the sale was finalized with a gesture of thanks. But it didn't end there!

I couldn't wait to tell her that God loved her.

"He proved His love for you by showing your physical condition to me in a dream. In the dream you showed me the large burn scars on your leg as a result of a car accident."

In the middle of relating to her the dream, she began crying uncontrollably and turned to her husband and said, "Tell them. Tell them. Please tell them about my car accident."

As he shared with us the account of the accident, the woman showed to us the large burn scars on her leg. She cried and was convinced that God must truly love her to have given a stranger a dream about her physical condition.

Now I knew why the Lord revealed this dream. It was an open door to the woman's heart. She was ready. This was a perfect setting for the Lord to work. His wonders never cease to amaze me.

We began to share the Word and the love of God with her. I quoted John 3:16: "For God so loved the world, that He gave His only begotten Son, that whosoever believeth in him should not perish, but have everlasting life." I told her, "Jesus, the Son of God, loved us enough to die on the cross for our sins, and He bore our sicknesses. We have forgiveness of our sins through His shed blood. All you have to do is confess Jesus as the Son of God and repent of your sins, receive Him into your heart, and make Him the Lord of your life. God can heal and restore you back to health, but more important than the healing of the body is the healing and Salvation of the soul." This was new to her, but she was ready to receive Christ into her heart.

This took place in a wonderful setting. We were outdoors, breathing the clean country air, with the bright blue sky and soft cotton-like clouds overhead. The sun was shining upon us, and as the Bible tells us, the angels in Heaven must have been rejoicing as Mrs. Moore led the woman in the Sinner's Prayer. The woman was so overwhelmed with joy. The presence of the Lord had shown all over her countenance.

Our mission was not over yet. I looked at her husband, a rather quiet man. He seemed to have an expression of approval about his wife's conversion experience.

I turned to him and said, "On this special day, I don't want to leave here without giving you the opportunity to accept Christ into your heart."

No sooner had I spoken these words that he immediately responded, "Yes, I also want Christ to come into my heart."

We sealed his commitment with a prayer. And then in unison we gave thanks to the Lord for our new brother and sister in Christ. We gave them directions to a full-gospel church and recommended that they attend the church where they would have fellowship, be instructed and grow in the ways of the Lord.

Oh, about the antique canning jar --was I foolish to sell them for only 14 dollars when just one rippled-blue glass jar was worth more than 14 dollars? Did I lose my earthly treasure, the canning jars, or did Mrs. Moore and I gain an eternal treasure by winning two new souls to the Lord?

My mother's wishes while she was on this earth were not for material possessions. Her desire and prayer was to see souls saved and come into the kingdom of God. If she were there when this event happened, she would had been pleased that I did not follow the dictates of my carnal mind, but rather the leading of the Holy Spirit.

Little did I know that the sale of my canning jars would be the vehicle that God would use to save two souls. That was when I understood the meaning of what the Holy Spirit had said, *"Your canning jars will still be your treasure."* Yes, my heavenly treasure!

I would like to leave you with this thought. One soul is worth more than the whole world to the Lord. The saying goes, "Tell me where your heart is, and I'll tell you where your treasures are." Is your heart on earthly treasures that are temporal or is your heart on heavenly treasures that are eternal?

In life we treasure many things: time, finances, recognition, relationships and sentimental objects. Do we value these things above our relationship with Christ? If not, then we should be willing to sacrifice anything for the cause of Christ.

Our Way or His Way

My husband, John, was organizing a trip to the Holy Land with a group of 32 people. The trip included five countries: Israel, Jordan, Italy, Switzerland and the last stop was Austria. Our son John David had already planned on joining the group.

They asked me to go with them on the trip, but truthfully, I had no desire to go. Some of my readers might question my decision. You must be thinking, "How could she miss out on such a wonderful opportunity that happens once in a lifetime!"

You may be right if you're thinking about the historical sites relating to Biblical events. I have always thought of the Lord as being in me and with me 24 hours a day. Therefore, I never felt the need to go to the Holy Land thousands of miles away to feel His presence in a more profound way.

I told my husband how I felt about the trip. He listened to me for a moment, and then said, "Did you pray before making your decision?"

"No, I guess you're right; I made my own decision without consulting God about it." A scripture verse came flashing in my mind, "In all of thy ways acknowledge him, and he shall direct thy paths." (Proverbs 3:6).

A sense of guilt came over me. I began praying, "Lord, I did not include you in my decision; please forgive me for not obeying your word. If you want me to go for whatever reason, I will put aside my own reasoning and I will go." Then a wonderful old song kept ringing in my ear. *"I'll go where you want me to go, dear Lord, I'll do what you want me to do, dear Lord, I'll say what you want me to say, dear Lord, I'll be what you want me to be."*

I asked the Lord for a witness to confirm what I was to do. Then one night, several days later, I had a dream that a man approached me and said, "You will travel to a far-off land and you will witness to a man about Jesus, even as Philip of old." Then the man disappeared from my dream and I was awakened.

The dream was so vivid in my mind. My answer came in that dream. I had to go God's way, not my way! When I submitted my will to God's will a profound peace and excitement came over me like a flood and saturated my whole being. My attitude changed and I was excited about going. Now, I had a purpose for going on the trip. I had a mission to accomplish for the Lord. I would meet someone and witness to that person about the Lord Jesus Christ. Now the trip took on a whole new meaning for me.

Preparations were being made and informative meetings were held. Our trip was ready to begin. Our first stop was Jordan. We viewed and enjoyed the religious and historical landmarks. As we were departing from Jordan, our Jordanian tour guide gave my husband a chocolate candy bar as a peace offering to give to our next tour guide who was from Israel.

Because of the endless disagreements and wars between their two countries, the two guides were not allowed to speak to each other. The hostility that existed between the two countries baffled my mind. To think that Jesus, the Prince of Peace, lived, walked and ministered in their lands, and yet such unrest and tumult existed between the two countries. But not surprisingly so, because they have rejected the Prince of Peace as the Son of God, Jesus, and Savior of the world. How can they have any lasting peace?

As we traveled throughout their land and walked along the shores of Galilee, we could feel and sense the awesome presence of God, permeating everything around us: the air, the sky and the very ground that we walked on. What a privilege it must have been to live in the land where Jesus lived while on earth, performing miracle after miracle. Oh that more of these blessed people would come to know the Savior of the world, Jesus, the son of the living God! We were sharing these beautiful thoughts as we left Jordan and entered into Israel.

We started with our new tour guide. He was very informative, sharing with us the biblical happenings that took place at the various locations. As we traveled with our Christian friends who came from different parts of the United States, the atmosphere on the bus was filled with harmonious singing of praises unto the Lord.

The tour guide was very moved by the words of the songs. He expressed that he sensed such a joy about our group. He said, "Why are you people so happy?" We prayed with him and introduced him to the Lord.

We arrived at the Upper Room where my husband ministered the Word. Together we all partook of the Lord's Supper. I was humbled that the Lord used me in this Holy place to bring forth a Word of Knowledge. Our guide told us later that evening at the hotel that he never witnessed such a wonderful presence of God before. He went on to say, "I have worked with many groups, but I had never before witnessed what has happened at the Upper Room today. I will never forget it."

From there we flew to Italy. We started the tour with an Italian guide, a wonderful middle-aged, woman. We traveled to historic Rome with all the wonderful, breathtaking sites including the fabulous cathedrals, with great works of art and unbelievable architecture. What talent God has endowed humans with throughout the ages!

Between viewing the sites, as we traveled by bus, our group continued to minister in song. Some of us spoke Italian and knew some of the Italian hymns. I suggested we sing an Italian hymn. The title of the song in English was, *"Come, my soul does seek thee, Oh Blessed Savior."* Our Italian tour guide was so moved and touched by this glorious hymn. She began to cry and said, "I have never heard such beautiful words." My husband shared with her the message of salvation and told her how much God loves her. With an open heart she repeated the Sinner's Prayer. At the end of the prayer, she said, "I felt a wonderful peace come over me. Thank you for introducing Jesus to me." We all were rejoicing over the Salvation of our dear Italian tour guide.

She told us she was facing very serious eye surgery. We prayed about her sickness and told her to keep believing for her healing miracle. We reminded her that God already gave her the most important miracle, the Salvation of her soul and the gift of eternal life. We encouraged her to find a full gospel church where she could grow in her walk with the Lord.

As our tour with her came to an end, we said our good-byes, and traveled back to our hotel, praising God for what had taken place. Through all the excitement my husband had forgotten to give the tour guide her tips. With this excuse he called her at her home. She was so elated when she heard his voice and said, "Sir Franco, I was just on my knees thanking Jesus for coming into my heart this day. Also, I must tell you, I have worked as a tour guide for many years, and no one has ever told me about Jesus and His great love for me. I cannot thank you enough. I feel like a new person. Now I know what real joy is."

With all the witnessing that took place, some of which I had a part in, I still felt I had not met or witnessed to the man in my dream. After going to Florence and Venice, we traveled by train to Switzerland for sightseeing and to attend the World Pentecostal Conference. There we met some of our fellow ministers and friends. It was an inspiring experience and an unforgettable blessing.

From there we went to Austria. It was our final stop before heading back to the states. At the airport we had many hours of waiting before our flight would leave. As I sat in the airport lobby, I quietly said to the Lord, "*I know the dream I had was from you, but I have not met the man I was to witness to.*" I did not hear a response from the Lord. I started to experience discouragement even though I had enjoyed the miraculous trip and all that happened.

I was sitting by myself, feeling sad, when one of the ladies in our group approached me and asked me to join her and go to the shopping center of the airport terminal. I refused her at first saying, "I have no interest in buying anything."

She said, "You don't have to buy anything. We have a long wait; it will do you good to get away for a while." Realizing the long wait ahead of us, I decided to go with her.

As we entered a crystal and glass gift store, the woman with me said, "Mrs. Franco, I would like to introduce you to the owner of this store." She had met him earlier with other members of our group.

As soon as I placed my eyes upon him, the Holy Spirit said, *"This is the man to whom you will witness."*

As I met him, the first thing he said to me was, "What do you think of my Jordanian people? Do you think they are bad people?" I immediately responded, *"What do I think of them? God loves them and I love them also. But one thing I cannot understand is that they cannot get along with their neighboring country Israel. To think that Jesus, the Prince of Peace, loved all of you so much that He came and dwelt among you, healing the sick, preaching and teaching the Word of God; yet there is no peace among you."*

I told him about the incident of the chocolate bar exchanged by us from the Jordanian guide to the Israeli guide. He was moved with emotion, almost in disbelief. I then shared with Him the message of salvation. I showed him the Bible that the woman with me had in her purse. I told him how the Old Testament spoke about a Messiah coming. The New Testament confirmed that the Messiah had come into the world and took upon Him the form of man. His name is Jesus. He lived a sinless life, fulfilling the will of His Father, was crucified, suffered pain and shed His blood by which we can have forgiveness of our sins. He died and rose again after three days and now He sits at the right hand of God interceding for you and for me.

Then I opened the Bible and read the following words of Jesus as found in the Bible. (John 14:6) "I am the way, the truth, and the life: no man cometh unto the Father, but by Me." (John 3:16) "For God so loved the world, that he gave his only begotten Son, that whosoever believeth in Him should not perish, but have everlasting life." (I John 1:9) "If we confess our sins, He is faithful and just to forgive us our sins, and to cleanse us from all unrighteousness." I told him, *"When I return home, I will mail you a Bible of your own."*

But immediately the woman with me said, *"No, he can have our Bible. It was my husband's Christmas gift, but I know he will be more than happy to leave it with him."*

I told him how much the Lord loved him and wanted to give him His peace, joy and eternal life. With this he said, "Yes, I want what you are telling me about. What do I have to do to receive what you have?" We prayed and led him to the Lord. He cried as I gave him the Bible, and he put it against his chest, embraced it and said, *"This is the best day of my life. I will treasure this book and read the scriptures you have given me to read."* As we were praying, the Lord spoke to me and said, *"Tell him that he will go back to his people and share the message of salvation and many will come to know the Lord through his testimony."*

I gave him this message from the Lord, and with tears in His eyes he looked at us and said, *"Yes, my people need to hear this message. Please pray for me."* Again we prayed for God's anointing upon his life and his future ministry.

How did I feel after this? I experienced great joy and fulfillment because I obeyed the Lord by submitting to His will. If not, I would have missed the opportunity of winning this Jordanian man to the Lord.

This precious soul, whose first name was Rajesh, said, *"Here is my business card. Please, keep in touch with me, and when I come to America for my import-export business, I will visit with you."* For some unknown reason this has not happened. I wrote to him three times since 1985 using the address on his business card, but each time the letter returned marked, "insufficient address." We wanted to keep our promise of keeping in touch, but maybe this was the extent of our friendship, just to plant the seed of salvation and then let God take over. For all that we know, he may have left his store in Austria and gone back to his people. We trust that wherever he is, he is witnessing and serving God. We look forward to meeting him again someday, if not here, then in glory.

Was it worth the trip across the ocean, thousands of miles away from home just to win one soul to the Lord? My answer is yes; for one soul is worth more than the whole world to the Lord, and we have no idea how many souls will be saved through this one man.

Our way or his way, our prayer should always be, "Lord not my will but Your will be done." This should be our prayer for every decision we have to make in our daily lives.

Come Destroy the Walls

At our church in Youngstown, Ohio, we held prayer meetings on Wednesday evenings. Our prayer meetings started with a silent time of self-introspection, dismissing anything that would inhibit our communication with God. It was a time and place where we could enter into His courts with praise and thanksgiving, worshipping the Lord in spirit and in truth. At this level of worship we were open to the movement of the Holy Spirit, where God could manifest Himself through a vision, prophecy or a Word of Knowledge.

During one of the prayer meetings different individuals were taking turns praying audibly. I was silently worshipping God in prayer when suddenly a vision opened up before me. In the vision, I saw myself kneeling with my head down on a bench. A wooden table was set in front of me. The Lord was in my vision, standing behind me. He began to speak to me in an audible voice. He said, "My child, look up." As I lifted my head and looked up toward the table, I noticed there were many cylinders. They were all different in size. Some had thick walls and some had narrow walls. Some were tall and some small.

Then the Lord spoke to me for the second time, *"My child look again."* As I looked closer, I saw small images inside each cylinder.

At first I thought, "What are these small images I am seeing? They look like ants?" My curiosity caused me to look again, but this time I leaned forward to have a better view of these images. As I looked, to my surprise I realized they were real people barely recognizable inside these walls. The people were so small compared to the thick tall walls that were built around them. The Lord spoke again for the third time and said, *"Men have divided my people by their interpretation of my Word. I will come, destroy the walls and unite my people once again."* With these profound Words the Lord disappeared and the vision was gone.

The vision had a twofold meaning. First, I believe the vision was an answer to a question I labored with for many years. And secondly, the vision came to open the spiritual eyes and attitudes of many Christians towards other denominations.

First, I want to share with you the question I had before the Lord since the age of 12. Back then while living in Long Island, I had a girlfriend in school by the name of Alice. We lived in a small town. There were only two churches, a Catholic Church and a full gospel Protestant Church. These churches were located within about 400 feet from each other. At the Protestant Church that I attended, we were told not to fellowship with the unsaved, while at the Catholic Church they were told not to fellowship with the Christians. If they did, they would be excommunicated from the church.

Alice and I were schoolmates. Our friendship was limited to walking to and from school and classroom interaction. Due to the religious attitude that existed at that time, we lived in fear that someone might see us walking together and report it to the priest or to my minister. If this were to happen, I would be reprimanded and Alice would be excommunicated from her church.

Even at that early age I couldn't understand why this attitude existed between the two churches. In my Sunday school class I was taught that we should love our neighbors. In my simplicity I thought, "Shouldn't we be demonstrating the love of God to them and overlooking their closed mindedness? Instead, we were isolating ourselves from them and creating walls of animosity between us. I thought, "There must be people behind those closed doors who love God in the only way they know how." I finally came to the realization through this vision that not God but people have created walls bringing about hatred and division among people and families. This attitude was so prevalent that we experienced isolation and discrimination because of our religious beliefs.

I knew that as long as I kept my faith and belief in God, there wasn't anything wrong in having a Catholic friend and sharing God's love. This is what I thought we should be doing as Christians, letting our light shine in a world of darkness.

On the other side of the coin, my family was ridiculed and criticized for years because my dad, a businessman who was highly esteemed among the town officials, changed from Catholicism to Christianity in a town where Catholicism was dominant. Thank God, we had a godly mother who told us never to retaliate because people didn't understand what they are doing.

Finally I thought I'd better tell my pastor about my friendship with Alice before someone else does. My pastor listened to me for a moment and then pointed toward heaven and said, "Look up to God." That answer did not satisfy my inquiry.

Months later, Alice's dad became a believer and started to attend our church. All hell broke loose in his family. His wife and children were strict Catholics. They disowned their father and put him out of the house because he became a believer. He went to live in his small barbershop about 200 feet away from his home. It was a two-room shack. When I heard this, I couldn't believe it! I thought, "How can a family mistreat their father and hold such animosity against him because he chooses to worship God in another way."

But there was something different about Alice compared to the rest of her family. She had compassion and love for her dad. She was the only one in the family who would care enough to bring her dad meals every morning and evening. I recall each day walking to school, waiting for Alice to bring a hot breakfast to her dad. She faithfully would check to see how he was doing. If he did not answer immediately, she would call out to him, "Papa, are you all right. Please open the door. It's Alice!"

She gave him the hot breakfast, and with an expression of joy he would say, "Thank you my daughter, God bless you." What an act of love and kindness!

I thought, "God, you must really love Alice for the way she takes care of her dad when everyone else in her family has disowned him. God, if you love Alice shouldn't I love her too?" The question in my mind still remained unanswered.

Later on in life we both went our separate ways. Alice went into the workplace and I continued my schooling. Eventually we both married. It happened that my husband hired Alice's husband, a carpenter, to do some work for us. With this we renewed our friendship. Our fun time together was crabbing, then ending the evening with a delicious crab dinner.

Several times we reminisced about the past. Alice told us about her dad passing away. She went on to say, "Your church had shown my dad so much love. They visited him, brought him meals and even gave him a new suit and shoes that he had on at his funeral. When everyone had forsaken my dad, your church people were there for him."

She began asking me many questions about our faith. She listened very attentively as I shared the Word of God with her. Then she said, "Rose, I always knew there was something different about you. That's why I enjoyed having you as my friend." I knew she wanted what I had. But her husband's negative attitude toward the things of God held her back from accepting the Lord.

Alice's family grew. They had several children, and everything in her family seemed to be going well until an unexpected circumstance changed their lives. Her husband became involved with a young lady, and the next thing we heard was that he left Alice and her children. What a tragedy! Her good marriage came crashing down. Her dreams for a good future had vanished. Alice's life completely changed. With all her disappointment and suffering she had to work and raise her children without a father. We were away in the ministry while all this had taken place.

After many years we moved back to Long Island. I called Alice and Mary, another classmate, and arranged for us to meet for breakfast. As usual when old friends meet after many years, the first thing we did was talk about our families and show photos. As Mary was showing us photos of her children, she began to cry as she told us, "This photo is of my oldest son, who was killed in a head-on car collision going to work one morning. It happened near my home, and every time I pass the scene of the accident I can't help but break down. He had a great future ahead of him, but his life was taken from him."

To my amazement, before I could give Mary some comforting words from the Lord, Alice began to tell Mary, "Jesus loves you and understands your sorrow. Turn your life over to Him. He alone can help you pull through this tragedy. Your son is in the hands of the Lord. Trust God and he will heal your broken heart. I know because He helped me overcome my heartache."

Can you imagine what went through my mind when I heard this? Alice must be a born-again Christian after all these years. I turned to Alice and said, "What wonderful encouraging words you had for Mary."

She looked at me and said, "I don't know what I would have done without the Lord. He sustained me after my husband left me. I have been attending a wonderful Protestant church where I received Jesus as my Lord and Savior, and my life has never been the same. Rose, I never forgot your friendship and the love shone to me when the odds were against us as young children. I always remembered the wonderful things about God that you and your husband shared with my ex-husband and me. I was seeking to find the peace and joy that you had and finally I found it in Jesus, the Prince of Peace."

Earlier in our friendship, Alice held back because of her husband, but the seeds that were sown were not in vain. For the Lord, who knew Alice's future, planted those seeds, the Word of God in her heart, so that they would grow and germinate and bring her into the full blooming stage of becoming a child of God at the right time in her life.

I trust you can understand why this vision meant so much to me. There had to be a divine reason why I was a friend to Alice, an unbeliever, in spite of the religious opposition. You can see through the course of events how God used our friendship and the love that was demonstrated toward Alice as a foundation that later led her to the Lord.

Scripture tells us that we are in the world but not of the world. Let's face it, however, we are in this world. We must work for a living, we are involved in our children's school activities, and some of us have unsaved relatives. I believe that, "not of this world" means that we, as followers of Christ should not have any part in the sinful practices and behavior of the world. God so loved the world (referring to the sinner) that He gave His only Son. We also must love and fellowship with the sinner, but have no part of their sinful practices. In doing so our light will shine in the midst of darkness and our witnessing to the unbeliever will be effective as stated in Matthew 5:16, "Let your light so shine before men, that they may see your good works, and glorify your Father which is in heaven." And in Romans 12:2 we read, "And be not conformed to this world, but be ye transformed by the renewing of your mind that ye may prove what is that good, and acceptable, and perfect, will of God."

I believe that God is destroying manmade walls and uniting people together who want the truth of God's Word, not in part, but the whole truth according to the scriptures. They are tired of man's formal and traditional religious beliefs and interpretations of the Bible. Therefore, God destroys the walls made by people and reaches out to a spiritually starving generation.

The second meaning of this vision became renewed again when my husband went to a minister's meeting held in upstate New York. After supper he shared with me one of the topics that was discussed at the meeting. He went on to say that at Notre Dame, a Catholic University, a revival had broken out and the people were receiving the baptism in the Holy Spirit. The sentiment was "How can this happen in a Catholic University? We have to be careful because we don't know if their experience is real."

When I heard this, the vision I had in Ohio came before me. I immediately told my husband, "John, do you recall the vision I had about the Lord destroying the manmade walls? We cannot agree with this sentiment. If we are not reaching these people who are hungry for more of God, He will go beyond the man made walls and reach them where they are. We need to be open to what God wants to do. People's ways are not God's ways. Time will tell."

Little did we know what God was about to do with our congregation just months later. Our Sunday morning service started at 10:30. Before we knew it, many Catholics were attending their mass at their early morning service and then hurrying down to attend our 10:30 service.

My husband and I were rejoicing over what God was doing. Remembering the vision, we both accepted them in love for we knew God was tearing down the walls of man. Not long after, some of our officers in the church began questioning the presence of these wonderful people. Here again, the question arose among them "We need to be careful. They are still going to their Catholic Church."

My husband responded to their concerns and answered, "Our doors are open to everyone. Who are we to judge them? Let's embrace them and accept them in the name of the Lord and the Lord will do the rest." There were about 45 Catholics who were attending our services. After hearing the Word of God preached, within a few weeks they stopped going to the Catholic Church and attended our services faithfully. They were so hungry for the truth of God's Word and readily accepted the Lord.

These precious souls began to grow and mature in the Lord. Many became helpers in the church. The greatest miracle, second to Salvation, was that about six of them dedicated their lives to the

Lord's work and are ministering today. What if we would have turned these wonderful souls away from our doors?

Remember the words of Jesus, "I will come destroy the walls and unite my people once again." This is so evident today.

These walls effect denominations and individuals. Some ministries today that are breaking down walls among the Christian denominations and uniting people of different faiths for the cause of Christ are Promise Keepers and Women of Faith.

Then there are individuals that are confined within the walls of religious tradition who are seeking after a deeper relationship with God. They break through the denominational wall and seek out a place of worship where the fullness of God's Word is preached feeding their spiritual hunger.

People have changed the meaning of God's Word by their own interpretation, but God has not changed and His Word is the same yesterday, today and forever.

Denominations and names will not save anyone of us. Only accepting Christ as Savior, keeping His commandments, and doing the will of the Father will assure us a place in heaven.

Chapter Eight

OUT OF BODY EXPERIENCE

———

Transported to Heaven

Our first full-time ministry position was in Youngstown, Ohio. A short time after we arrived there, the church members decided to sell the building. Unexpectedly, within only a few weeks the old church building sold. Not long after that, the Lord provided a beautiful parcel of ground with an English Colonial house and enough land to build a church.

Our next challenge was to find a place of worship while our new church was being built. Fortunately, a school allowed us to use their building for our Sunday and Wednesday services.

During the transitional period, prayer meetings were held in the homes of church members. One night, at a prayer meeting we were all kneeling down when my husband started the prayer time by singing several choruses. I was praying with my face down on the couch, when suddenly I lost all feeling in my body. I felt lifeless. My soul left my body and began ascending upward. It felt as though I was in my body, but at the same time, I felt as light as a feather. My arms were straight down against my body, but my hands and feet were flapping forward and backwards.

I was not traveling alone; Jesus was at my side. Around Him was a beam of light that dispelled the darkness around us. We were traveling at an extremely fast rate of speed. There was no exchange of words between the Lord and myself as we soared through the skies.

We arrived at our destination. There was an entrance to this glorious incredible place called heaven. It was far beyond my wildest imagination. There was no darkness to be seen anywhere. The bright light permeated everywhere and it shone over everything. It was so quiet and peaceful. The atmosphere created a feeling of serenity.

Everything was transparent. As I looked in from the outside, I saw my mother. She was sitting on a bench, but yet it did not look like any material that would be familiar to us on earth. Even the bench looked transparent. My wonderful mother had a peaceful look upon her face.

Then I recognized another relative standing at a distance. I was so happy to see that she made heaven. I looked at the Lord and wanted to tell Him how happy I was. But I knew by His expression that He didn't want me to talk. Instead, without any verbal utterance, He gave me a message to bring back to earth. The message from our Lord was, *"Be still, my child. I have brought you here only to show you that heaven is real. Go back and tell others what you have seen."*

In a flash, my soul was back into my earthly body. I was speechless for awhile. I felt so humble to think that the Lord had chosen me among others to see this beautiful place called heaven. It was a preview of our final destination.

In the past, I heard about other Christians having similar experiences. Some of you reading about this encounter may wonder, "Can this really happen to us mortal, imperfect human beings?" I can understand why some people find it hard to believe that these experiences are real.

Do I doubt the testimonies of others that have experienced heaven whether in a dream, vision or reality? No, not even for a moment. I know that God loves us so much that He reveals Himself to us through His Word, dreams, visions and heavenly experiences. The Lord wants us to be aware that there is a real hell to shun and *a real heaven to gain*.

I know that I know without a shadow of a doubt that there is a place called heaven. It is beautiful, peaceful and almost indescribable. This experience has encouraged me to witness and share Christ with others. Heaven is real. What I saw in heaven confirms what the Scripture says about heaven.

Jesus told the disciples in John 14:2-3, "In my Father's house are many mansions: if it were not so, I would have told you. I go to prepare a place for you. And if I go to prepare a place for you, I will come again, and receive you unto myself; that where I am, there ye may be also."

This place called heaven is prepared for all those who have accepted Christ, repented of their sins and have served the Lord.

Life is but a vapor. It comes and goes. The day will come for each one of us to face our eternal destination. We have two choices, either heaven or hell. When heaven's roll call is read, will we hear "Come, ye blessed of my Father, inherit the kingdom prepared for you.." (Matthew 25:34b) or will He look upon us and say, "Depart from me, ye cursed, into everlasting fire, prepared for the devil and his angels:" (Matthew 25:41b). Whom will you serve? The choice is yours.

The day is nearing. If we truly know and love the Lord, we will draw near unto Him and seek His will for our life as we make preparation for His return. If you do not know Him as the Lord and Savior of your life, do not wait any longer. Ask Jesus to come into your heart, forgive you of all your past sins and make you a child of God. With His help you can live an overcoming life in a world of darkness.

One day soon and very soon we are going to see the King of Kings and Lord of Lords, whether it is individually or whether we meet Him in the clouds of glory when He returns for the church, His bride. "I must work the works of him that sent me, while it is day: the night cometh, when no man can work." (John 9:4).

Yes, I know there is a place, with unexplainable beauty, of quiet rest, where there is no suffering, and there is no night there, for all is light. How can I ever forget the words of Jesus, *"Be still, my child. I have brought you here only to show you that heaven is real. Go back and tell others what you have seen."*

Is there a mansion waiting for you in heaven? I'll be looking for you when the roll is called up yonder at our eternal destination called heaven.

Chapter Nine

MOTHER'S JOURNEY-START TO FINISH

A Mother's Reflection of Christ

"Who can find a virtuous woman? For her price is far above rubies." (Proverbs 31:10). "Her children arise up, and call her blessed; her husband also, and he praiseth her." (Proverbs 31:28).

I attribute my love for the Lord to my earthly mother. She was the greatest influence on my spiritual life. We grew up being exposed to her Christ-like example that was manifested in her everyday life. She lived what she professed. There was no compromising with the Word of God. The word "discrimination" was never used in our home. All people were God's creation, regardless of race, color or creed, and we were to show God's love to everyone and treat them all the same.

As I share some of Mother's life with you, I'm sure you will agree that she had to have a strong faith and a deep relationship with God in order to handle the adverse hardships of her life. She never complained, but she carried her cross with joy. The joy of the Lord gave her the strength to endure and to hurdle over every obstacle.

My mother was 28 years old when my dad, 32 years of age, came down with an unexpected prolonged sickness. We were looked upon by the world's standards as the ideal, successful and comfortable family who came to America, worked hard and made it big. But all our popularity and earthly achievements came to a halt due to this intruder called sickness.

Suddenly the sun stopped shining. The raging storms of life had obscured its visibility. How was Mother ever going to pull through this unforeseen circumstance? Would she be able to see the sun shine again? Not within her limited capabilities and strength. She certainly was not prepared to handle this catastrophe. She was thrust into an insurmountable situation, having to shoulder the responsibility of caring for and raising five young children without her husband. Her meager income came from Dad's concrete cement block business. He did not carry disability insurance to compensate for the loss of income during an illness.

Prior to Dad's illness, my mother never had to work. Dad was a good provider. He was a firm believer that the wife's duty was to stay at home and care for her children. Therefore, she was never involved in any aspects of my dad's business.

When illness strikes, it affects the whole family structure, bringing about many changes and adjustments in order to survive. Mother had to take on a twofold responsibility. In the family structure, she no longer played the role of a sweet, tender, overprotective mother and housewife, but now she had the additional responsibility of running a concrete block business.

To meet the financial needs of the family, she had to adjust to the business world by taking over a strenuous man's job. Out of necessity and the love for her children, she quickly had to learn how to make cement blocks. She would manually shovel cement into block forms and operate the large electrical block maker.

Before my brother was able to drive, Mother drove the old truck and delivered the blocks to the customers. She spoke very little English, but she never gave up. She tried her hardest to communicate with the workers and the customers.

Her additional role of running a company didn't interfere with her motherly love and care for her children. She was up at dawn each day, making a hot breakfast for us, preparing our clothes and seeing us off to school. As we arrived home from school, we were greeted with the aroma of fresh homemade bread. Every evening we all sat around the table and enjoyed a full dinner made by Mother's labor of love.

She worked feverishly at washing our clothes with an old-fashioned wringer-type washing machine that oftentimes would break down. Dad wasn't there to repair it, so she would take it apart and try to fix it herself.

There was a time when we were hurting financially. I had only one hand-me-down dress to wear. I remember my mother leaning over the sink, washing that dress by hand so it would be clean for the next day.

Before Dad's illness, he had many friends in the political and in the business world. In the house that Dad built, he had constructed an entertainment room about 40 feet long. This room was used once a month to entertain his friends. He served them a delicious dinner, followed by a night of fun, dancing and entertainment.

Prior to Dad's illness he was exposed to the Christian faith. A couple had witnessed to him about Jesus and gave him a Bible. He brought the Bible home and read it every day. New truths were revealed to him that he had never heard before. He began sharing these truths with my mother and other relatives. Mother was taught that the Catholic Church was the only true universal church. She was fearful of change or of accepting any other religious belief. She told my dad, "I was born a Catholic and I will remain a Catholic until I die." This strong statement changed not long after Dad's illness.

The support and comfort she needed after Dad's illness did not come from Dad's worldly friends. It came from the Christians that Dad had met. God's love manifested through these people touched my mother's heart and she accepted Christ and the Christian faith.

Her relationship and love for the Lord grew with each passing day. The Word of God was planted in her heart. The Lord became first in her life and then the love for her husband and five children. As we were growing up, her Christian walk influenced our relationship with God. She took time from her busy schedule to teach us the ways of the Lord and His commandments. In our home, there was always a spirit of love, joy, contentment and loving discipline when needed.

Not long after Mother's conversion, a new church was started in our home. A minister was called in to hold services. Mother's car was used to transport people to the meetings. The church membership grew. Property was donated and a church building was built on a main highway. It all started because one woman put God and His work before her own needs and hardships. Because of her dedication, many souls came to know the Lord.

Christ became the head of our home. Many times Mom would tell us, "Remember, your earthly father cannot be with you, but your heavenly Father is always with you. He sends His angels to watch over you." She instilled within our conscience an awareness of God. We were taught that pleasing and obeying God should be out of love for Him and not out of fear.

Her love and concern for the needs of the less fortunate was an example to us. Even though there were times when we did not have enough money to pay bills or buy the bare necessaries of life, Mother still gave to others. When times were bad, Mother would call us together to pray and trust God to supply our needs.

I recall one time during the cold winter months when cement blocks were not selling and no monies were coming in, Mother had us pray about our financial need. That very next day, of all people, a customer who owed an old pass due bill that was written off the books as a noncollectable debt, came to our home with five hundred dollars! All the correspondence and phone calls could not retrieve this money, but through prayer, God bypassed all human communication and touched the heart of this man to pay the debt he owed, and at the same time meeting our need. What is impossible with man is possible with God. Mother reminded us of the faithfulness of God. This miracle was only one of many provision miracles and answered prayers that we experienced in our childhood days. We were fortunate to have been exposed to a strong solid Christian foundation.

Mother taught us to have mercy, compassion, love and patience with each other and with other people. I will never forget her looking at us with her beautiful big hazel eyes and saying, "Never criticize, murmur or point your finger at others because when you do, three little fingers are pointing back at you." These words still linger in my heart today and I've passed them on to my children and grandchildren.

Mother's devotion and faithfulness to my dad in spite of his many years of illness were to be admired. In snow, rain or sunshine, she would cook for him and visit him twice a week traveling a distance of 15 miles one way. Never did she complain or blame God for my dad's illness, but with joy she carried her cross. She fought a good fight, held on to her faith and finished her race with triumph.

Her spiritual legacy was passed on to her five children, her grandchildren and great grandchildren who are all serving the Lord today.

As for myself, I loved my mother dearly and will always treasure her deep but simple godly advice and her faithful prayer life. She was a true example of a godly Christian mother. I will always remember her motto, "Jesus first, others second, and yourself last." Trials? Yes. Suffering? Yes. But through it all she was content with the provisions God provided for her and her family. Like the words in the song she often sang, "It will be worth it all when we see Jesus. Each trial will seem so small, when we see Him." Now she is enjoying her reward, her heavenly mansion with her Lord and Savior, Jesus Christ.

My Mother's Mansion

We were living at Kenmore, New York, outside of Buffalo. It was a bright sunny day in the month of March. As in the past, I would call my dear mother every Sunday afternoon to touch base with her.

On this particular Sunday as my mother answered the phone she began singing in her loving broken English language the words of a song that was dear to her heart. *"What a day that will be when my Jesus I shall see. When I look upon His face, the one who saved me by his grace, when he takes me by the hand and leads me to the promised land, what a day, glorious day that will be."* I couldn't help but join her in singing, knowing this was one of her favorite songs.

Mother had had diabetes and high blood pressure since her late thirties, but she never complained about her illness. I told her, "Mamma, I'm concerned about your physical health."

To put my mind at ease she said, "I don't want you to worry, Rosina. I will call and visit my doctor tomorrow."

Then she continued to tell me that the week before, many young people in her church had received the baptism in the Holy Ghost according to Acts 2:4. My mother always had a burden for the young people. She often said, "Remember, that the youth are the Church of tomorrow. We should show them love, understanding and compassion." With this good news we ended our phone conversation.

My son Johnny, 13 years of age at the time, had been outdoors playing when I phoned my mother. He was terribly disappointed that he missed Grandma's call.

He said, "Mom, you know how much I love Grandma. There is something I want to tell her."

Without hesitation I said, "I'm sorry son, I will call Grandma back again and you can speak to her."

As I said this, his big brown eyes lit up, and he was smiling from cheek to cheek. I knew the happiness that both my mother and Johnny would experience through this phone call.

When I called, Grandma was thrilled to hear her Johnny Boy's voice. Johnny went on complementing her good cooking and said, "My mom made lasagna today, but I like your lasagna a little better." He told Grandma how much he loved and missed her.

She replied, "I love you too, Johnny Boy. Be good and always look to Jesus." He then said his goodbye and handed the phone back to me.

My mother's last words were, "Rosina, I pray that God will always watch over you as you travel, and remember to always keep the joy of the Lord in your heart, for it is your strength. Stay close to the Lord. God bless you, Rosina, bella di Mamma." Little did I know this would be the last time Johnny and I would hear my mother's voice.

I learned later that my mother kept her promise to visit her doctor on the very next day. He gave her a clean bill of health and said, "You are doing fine, Mary." On her way home she stopped at the store to buy some fruit and vegetables, which were still on her kitchen table two days later. After having a light supper, she relaxed in her living room and made several calls to her Christian friends. We were told later that she had encouraged each of them in the Lord.

I am so proud to say my mother was always a peacemaker. She never indulged in murmuring or backbiting. She would remind people to keep their eyes on the Lord, because he is the only perfect one. After making her phone calls, she went to bed. Later that night she suddenly became very ill. She was experiencing severe pains in the stomach and in her chest.

Early the next morning I received a call from my sister, "Rose, Mom had to be rushed to the hospital. She had a massive heart attack." Immediately my husband made arrangements for my flight home.

He left me at the airport and returned home to get Johnny Boy off to school. The plane was scheduled to leave at 9:30 am. About 20 minutes before the flight was to leave, we were called to board the plane. At first everything seemed to be fine, but the plane was held up for quite awhile. Then a voice came over the loud speaker telling all passengers to please leave the plane and return to the airport terminal. I was upset and worried that I might not arrive in time to see my mother alive.

While waiting in the airport, I remembered my mother's last words as she prayed for me during our last phone conversation. She had asked the Lord to watch over me as I travel. I said to myself, "What does all this delay mean?"

Within minutes all passengers on our flight were asked to gather in a special room. Knowing that many of us were upset the captain said, "Please everyone be calm. If this plane had left the airport, none of you would have reached your destination. The plane has developed mechanical failure, and we do not have the parts needed to repair it. Therefore, we need to bring in another plane to accommodate all of you."

Now I knew why my mother prayed that prayer. I believe that God directed the captain not to fly the plane because of her prayers.

Never underestimate the effectiveness of a mother's prayer. Thank God for praying mothers.

We finally left the airport at 2:30 p.m., and all the way to New York City I prayed, "Lord let me arrive in time to see my mother once more before you call her home to Glory."

When we arrived at the hospital, I entered the lobby with my sister who had come up from Florida. I was anxious to get to my mother's room. I tried to bypass the information desk, but a clerk stopped me and asked for the patient's name and said, "Wait here. The supervisor wants to speak to you." I knew what this meant. I had missed seeing my wonderful mother alive by only 30 minutes. Her lifeless body was still in the room but we were not allowed to see her. The Lord did not grant me my heart's desire. I cannot describe in words how badly I was hurting. Being filled with grief and sorrow, all I could do was call out to God for comfort. My loving mother had gone to be with her Maker, the Lord and Savior of her life.

I was so disappointed. Her death was so sudden and unexpected. I just cried constantly asking God, "Why did I not have the honor of being with my mother during her last moments on earth? You know Lord, how much I loved, respected and cherished her. I wanted more then anything to be by her side when you called her home. Why Lord? Why?" At the time it seemed that the Lord was not hearing my agonizing prayer or aware of my heartache.

I wanted so badly to go to my mother's home, touch her clothes and sleep in her bed as I did in the past. The family insisted, "Mamma is not there; she is with the Lord."

They did not understand the deep bond I had with my mother. It was more of a spiritual connection. She would share with me her problems and say, "Rosina, I know you have compassion and understand my heartache." In agreement, we prayed about the need.

There were times we laughed together and times we cried. It is sad to say that many parents are not privileged to have a spiritual bond with their children where they can share their concerns and pray together. I thank God and feel privileged that I can share this same spiritual bond with my children.

That evening I stayed with another sister. I had no desire to eat. I just could not stop crying. It was time to go to sleep, but I was wide-awake. I had no intentions of sleeping. My sister begged me, "Please, Rose, try to get some sleep. Mamma would not want you to carry on like this. You know she is in heaven with the Lord."

I told my sister, "Okay, Jennie, I will close my eyes, but I can't sleep thinking about Mamma and why I didn't get to see her alive."

To my surprise, as I closed my eyes, I saw a very bright light from a distance. At first, I could not make out what it was. But gradually the image came closer, and I could see that it was my mother's heavenly mansion. The rooms were all transparent. You could see through each room. The beautiful colors were soft in hue. The beauty was indescribable.

As soon as the image became clear and recognizable, it vanished and I went into a deep sleep. I was the one who was not going to fall asleep, but something unexplainable happened. I recall that the light in my vision was so powerful and bright that I had to turn my face away from it. As I did this, I fell asleep. It was similar to someone receiving medication intravenously to put one to sleep. I believe God saw my sorrow and gave me the vision of my mother's mansion to comfort me. But He wasn't finished with me yet. In my sleep He visited me in a dream.

Everybody in the house was awake except me. They did not want to disturb me. But just before I awoke, the Lord gave me a dream about my mother. I dreamed she was on a potter's wheel, finishing a vessel that she had made. The room had two doors, one on the left side of the room and another door on the right side. A man dressed in white, which was Jesus, entered through the right door and looked at my mother as she was examining her vessel to see if it was ready. Seeing that it was incomplete, she was dissatisfied. The footing on the bottom and the trimming on the top of the vessel were not finished.

The Lord made a signal with his hand, "Come, we must go."

The expression on my mother's face seemed to be saying, "But Lord, I still have two more unfinished steps to complete before I can leave. Can you give me a little more time?"

The Lord nodded his head and motioned with his hand as if to say, "Okay my child, but we must hurry."

My mother completed the last two steps, and then looked at the vessel from all angles as she examined it for any imperfections. At that point she appeared to be happy. She smiled and nodded her head, saying, "Lord, I am ready now." Then Jesus walked up to her and put his arm around her and together they went out through the left door. I woke up from this dream rejoicing. All my crying, sorrow and heartache had ceased.

After I had this dream, I realized that God had given my mother the miracle that she had prayed for. Her desire was that God would take her home to glory quickly without a prolonged sickness. God answered her prayer. Just before the Lord called her home, she was wide-awake and fully conscious. When my sister visited our mother in her hospital room, she told her, "Kay, I put all my burial instructions and papers on my bedroom bureau before I left the house." Then she added, "I recommend that you love one another and that you keep in touch with your brother and sisters." These were her final words. I believe she prepared all the necessary documents because she knew the Lord was going to call her home.

After God had revealed this dream to me, I experienced a peace and joy that only He could give. I was convinced that God wanted me to remember my mother alive. He did not want me to see her dying. As I viewed her earthly body that was laid out at the funeral home, I could only envision her in her heavenly mansion, in the presence of the Lord. What a comforting thought! I will never forget that vision and the dream as long as I live on this earth.

Heaven is real, beautiful and so peaceful. I can't help remembering the words of the last song my mother sang during our last phone call, *"What a day that will be when my Jesus I shall see. When I look upon his face, the one who saved me by his grace, when he takes me by the hand and leads me to the promised land, What a day, glorious day that will be."* Jesus did meet her and walked her into the Promised Land. My mother's song became a reality.

The Lord was good to her by extending her time on earth to finish her vessel, leaving nothing undone. While on earth, she sent up treasures to her heavenly mansion. She was ready to meet her master, the Lord Jesus Christ.

We cannot avoid facing death one day. The question remains- *Are our vessels clean and ready to please the master?* Do we have unfinished business to take care of? *Will the Lord say to us on that final day, "Well done, my good and faithful servant, enter into the joy that is prepared for you?"* Let us be ready, with our lamps burning bright, for we know not the hour that our Lord will come for us.

Chapter Ten

WHY I BELIEVE IN THE HOLY SPIRIT

Why Did Jesus Send the Holy Spirit?

The Holy Spirit's presence has been my sustaining spiritual force. I experience Him in my life as Comforter, Spirit of Truth, protector, deliverer and teacher. After I received the baptism in the Holy Spirit, my source of spiritual power, and as I drew closer to God, the spiritual gifts began operating through my life. As you experience God beyond belief and enter into the supernatural realm of His spiritual promises, you will find that there isn't anything in this world that can compare with the joy and fulfillment it brings. In fact, you will live a more content and victorious life because your dependence rests on Him rather than yourself or on people.

I do not speak on the subject of the Holy Ghost as a research theologian but as a born-again child of God who believes the written Word of God and is filled with the Holy Spirit and power. I have witnessed firsthand the Holy Spirit's workings in action, resulting in a life of miracles.

I cannot understand or fathom in my limited knowledge why people do not see the need for the empowering promise of the infilling of the Holy Spirit that Jesus provided for the disciples and for the forthcoming generations.

Today there is a Holy Spirit renewal-taking place in our generation. An uprising of spiritual hunger is evident especially among our young people. Just empty form and rituals are not enough to satisfy their spiritual appetite. They are searching for the full revelation of what they are hearing and reading. Their cry is, "If Jesus Christ is the same yesterday, today and forever, then why aren't we experiencing the manifestation of the Holy Spirit and power in our lives and in our churches as the early church experienced?"

Early one morning as I thought upon this I found myself asking God a question similar to that of today's youth, "Why are there so many preachers of the gospel who do not believe in the infilling of the Holy Spirit as written in Acts 2:4?"

I'll never forget how clearly God responded to my question by saying, "*I did not leave my disciples comfortless and powerless, but in my stay, I sent them another comforter, the Holy Ghost, to abide with them forever, even the spirit of truth. He would teach them all things. This promise was not only for my disciples, but for all who believe, that they may receive power to see even greater miracles than I have done through the power of the Holy Ghost that would dwell within them. Blessed are they, who believe and seek for the promise, for they will be filled with the Holy Ghost and power. My child, even as thou are walking in the power of the Holy Spirit, thou have seen many miracles come to pass, continue therein and greater things will thou see with your eyes in the days ahead. Fear not and go forth in the power of My name for I am with thee; for in your obedience, thou has found favor in my sight.*"

How true, the promise was and is available to anyone who believes and seeks after it.

The key word is "believe" which means to take as true, or to trust as a promise. If preachers or Christians do not believe that the infilling of the Holy Ghost and power (as in Acts 2:4) is for today, how can they receive it? Many teach that the Acts 2:4 experience was only for the early church and that the Holy Spirit comes upon (which means alongside of, or near to) the believer when they accept Jesus Christ into their heart.

You might think about this example. I brought along an apple "with" me to work today and at lunchtime I "shall" (implies future) eat the apple. Only after I have eaten the apple can I say the apple is inside of me (abides, dwells, or resides "in" me) and my body receives its nutritional benefits.

This parable relates to the promise of the infilling of the Holy Spirit. Just like you can't enjoy the benefits of an apple until you have it inside of you, you can't receive the full benefit of the Holy Spirit until you receive the baptism in the Holy Spirit and it dwells within you.

Let us think about the disciples for a moment. I'm sure you agree with me that they were believers and followers of Christ. In John 14:17 we read, "Even the Spirit of truth, whom the world cannot receive, because it seeth him not, neither knoweth him: but ye know him; for he dwelleth with you, and shall be in you." If just having the Holy Spirit dwelling with them was enough to empower them to continue to do the work of Jesus then, what do we do with this scripture? It is very obvious to understand the words of Jesus when

He said, "he (now) dwelleth 'with' you, and 'shall' (future) be 'in' you." It is evident that the Holy Spirit did dwell "with" the disciples but Jesus promised them that it would not only be with them but that it shall be in them. Until the day of Pentecost, they did not have the infilling of the Holy Spirit residing within them. Then again in the book of John Jesus repeatedly spoke to the disciples using the words "shall" and "will" referring to a future time when they would receive the baptism of the Holy Spirit. Then in Acts 1:5, Jesus told the disciples, "For John truly baptized with water; but ye shall be baptized with the Holy Ghost not many days hence." We can not overlook Acts 1:8 when Jesus told the disciples, "But ye shall receive power, after that the Holy Ghost is come upon you: and ye shall be witnesses unto me both in Jerusalem, and in all Judea, and in Samaria and unto the uttermost part of the earth."

On the day of Pentecost, in the Upper Room, the disciples received the promise. They believed, obeyed and waited 120 in number, all in one place. Then, in one accord as they prayed, they were all baptized in the Holy Spirit with the evidence of speaking in an unknown tongue as the spirit gave them utterance, confirming the promise of Jesus. This promise was to be passed down to each forthcoming generation.

It is written that after the disciples and the early church received the indwelling of the Holy Spirit, they were empowered and anointed to carry on the ministry with signs and wonders. In the church today how much more do we need to be empowered by the indwelling of Holy Spirit to witness to the unsaved, to have access to the gifts of the Spirit and witness the miracle working power of God.

Think about this question, "If the baptism in the Holy Spirit could be received in any other way, why wouldn't Jesus have told us? But God chose to send the infilling of Holy Spirit on the day of Pentecost with the evidence of speaking with other tongues. This was in God's divine plan for humanity even as He chose for salvation to be available to the believer through the sacrifice of His son Jesus.

There is no question that as one draws closer to God and operates under the anointing of the Holy Spirit signs, wonders and miracles will result. In reading my book you will understand why I say that I am a witness to the Truth that greater things can be done in the name of Jesus through the power of the Holy Spirit that dwells within us.

The question remains in my heart, *"Lord, in these last days, will more Christians seek after and believe in the infilling of the Holy Spirit and power even as many of us have been blessed with this promise?"* I believe so, for the Word of God tells us in Acts 2:16,17, "But this is that which was spoken by the prophet Joel; 'And it shall come to pass in the last days, saith God, I will pour out of my Spirit upon all flesh:.."

There are so many different beliefs and interpretations on this subject, but I accept and choose to believe the Word of God as truth and that His promise of the Holy Spirit and the gifts are for today.

Miracles and wonders operate in the supernatural realm of our spiritual experience through the workings of the Holy Spirit. The manifestation of the Holy Spirit can take place in a church setting, a home, a hospital or wherever God chooses. If we quench the Spirit, the workings of the Holy Spirit and its gifts will not operate in our services.

My Heavenly Language

In my personal experience, when I was baptized in the Holy Spirit, I received my heavenly language that has played an important part in my spiritual life. In times of rejoicing and especially in times of sorrow, I have prayed in my heavenly language. When this happens, I do experience a greater closeness to God. I derive strength, encouragement and an intimacy that cannot be experienced in any other way. Remember this is one language that the enemy of our soul cannot understand and God many times uses our unknown language to come against Him.

Therefore, there is a purpose for the heavenly language in one's prayer life. Our Spirit becomes edified as we speak to the Lord in our own heavenly language. I like to think about it as my private secret prayer language that only the Lord and my spirit understand.

Recently on a Christian TV program, a well-known healing evangelist openly shared with the audience that, in his daily devotions, he prays in his heavenly language. I was not surprised after hearing the wonderful revelations God has given him and how God has used him mightily in his many years of ministry.

There is a difference between our personal heavenly language that comes when one receives the baptism in the Holy Spirit, as recorded in Acts 2:4, and that of the gift of tongues as mentioned in 1 Corinthians 12:10, which I will mention in the next section.

The Spiritual Gifts

The spiritual gifts are the manifestations of the Holy Spirit as we read in 1 Corinthians 12:4-7 NIV, "There are different kinds of gifts, but the same Spirit. There are different kinds of service, but the same Lord. There are different kinds of working, but the same God works all of them in all men. Now to each one of the manifestation of the Spirit is given for the common good."

There are nine gifts, all given by the same spirit. They are usually broken down in three categories:

Gifts of revelation, given to the church for leadership and teaching: the word of wisdom, the word of knowledge, the discerning of spirits;

Gifts of power, given for the ministry to the church: faith, the working of miracles, healing:

Gifts of utterance, given from God for communication with the church: prophecy, diverse kinds of tongues and interpretation of tongues. These spiritual gifts are given to every man as He wills.

The gift of diverse kinds of tongues is a message from God that sometimes precedes the interpretation of tongues. In 1 Corinthians 14:1 Paul instructs us, "Follow after charity, and desire spiritual gifts, but rather that ye may prophesy." He admonished the early church that if one speaks in an unknown tongue he speaks to God and edifies himself. But when one interprets the unknown tongue, then the message whether it be one of revelation, knowledge, prophesying or doctrine, will bring edification, exhortation and comfort to the church.

The Word of the Knowledge is a gift from the Holy Spirit that reveals some knowledge or information that the person bringing forth this message would normally not know. This can reveal a sickness, a prophecy, a warning, or a revelation for an individual or a church body.

God also reveals deeper things to us when the gifts of the Holy Spirit are operating. Many times miracles and workings of the Holy Spirit pass us by because of unbelief and the closed mindedness of the leaders. Jesus himself could not perform any great miracles in His own town because of unbelief. Unbelief holds back the working hand of God. Where there is freedom for the movement of God, we see many miracles taking place, not by man's doing, but by the Holy Spirit.

In 1 Corinthians 2:9-14 we read, "But as it is written, Eye hath not seen, nor ear heard, neither have entered into the heart of man, the things which God hath prepared for them that love him. But God hath revealed them unto us by his Spirit: for the Spirit searcheth all things, yea, the deep things of God. For what man knoweth the things of a man, save the spirit of man which is in him? even so the things of God knoweth no man, but the Spirit of God. Now we have received, not the spirit of the world, but the spirit which is of God; that we might know the things that are freely given to us of God. Which things also we speak, not in the words which man's wisdom teacheth, but which the Holy Ghost teacheth; comparing spiritual things with spiritual. But the natural man receiveth not the things of the Spirit of God: for they are foolishness unto him: neither can he know them, because they are spiritually discerned."

I believe the Word is very explicit. Man in his natural state can never understand or know the things of the spirit, therefore it is only by the Holy Spirit that the spiritual things of God are revealed and manifested.

When speaking about the gifts of the Holy Spirit, I firmly believe that they should be cultivated and executed in an orderly way at God's own timing and place. I found in my own experience, if God wants the Word of Knowledge or any other gift to come forth, He will make the way to bring it to pass as long as there is freedom for the Holy Spirit to operate. If not, then one must be silent.

Many answered prayers have come about while the gifts were operating in the church. During the manifestation of the gifts, I have personally witnessed many miracles through the ministering of the gifts. Some are included in this chapter and others are recorded throughout my book.

A Word of Knowledge Started a Revival

On a Saturday morning we traveled from Detroit, Michigan to our next meeting in New Jersey. We arrived at the hotel about eight o'clock in the evening. About nine o'clock the phone rang. It was the pastor of the church where we were to minister the next morning. He spoke to my husband about our accommodations and informed him of the service time. We had never met this pastor before, and this was our first time at this church.

We arrived at the church the next morning. My husband had asked me to set up his tapes while he was ushered into the pastor's study. I had not yet met the pastor or the assistant pastor. By the time

I finished setting up the tapes, the service had started. The congregation was standing while singing a chorus. I quietly was ushered to about the eighth row from the front of the church. There were about twelve hundred people in the service.

As usual I silently began praying, asking God to bless His people and the service. As I was praying, I heard a voice say, "You will bring forth a Word of Knowledge to my people, but I will not give you the message in tongues. You will only give the interpretation of the message." When I heard this, I began to tremble and said, "Lord, I want to obey you, but the pastor doesn't know who I am. It's my first time here, and I don't know if they operate in the Gifts of the Spirit. Lord, I want to obey you. Take away the spirit of fear and may the Holy Spirit anoint the words that come forth out of my mouth." After saying this, a woman in one of the back rows began to bring forth the message in tongues with a powerful voice.

I felt a hand push against my back, as if to say, "Go forth in the power of my name." Then immediately the message from the Lord came flowing freely from my mouth as I was still trembling. The Lord told me to say to them, *"You have removed the candlestick that I have placed before thee."* He went on to tell them that *He loved them but could not bless them because they had chosen to go their own way and not the way of the Lord.* This was a powerful message telling the people that God was displeased because they had quenched the moving of the Holy Spirit in their midst.

The pastor took the microphone from the song leader and told the people, "We all heard the message the Holy Spirit brought forth this morning. Let us continue to worship God and allow Him to have

His way in the service. I believe there's more that God wants to say to us. Let us all pray and wait upon God a little longer."

As we were standing and worshipping the Lord, the Holy Spirit spoke to me again: *"My child, go to the pulpit and share what I had given you at the Merritt Island church."* Immediately the article, "From Formalism to Fanaticism" came before me. It was not normal for me to walk up to the pulpit and say, "I have something the Lord wants me to share with you," especially when it is my first time at a church.

As I opened my eyes, the pastor had turned the service back to the song leader. Again I said, *"Lord go before me and give me the words to speak."* I approached the pulpit and told the song leader, "I'm Mrs. Franco. I have something the Lord wants me to share with the people."

He gladly said, "Please, sister, let the Lord lead you." I began giving forth the illustration with the emphasis on quenching the Holy Spirit.

Then the Holy Spirit inspired me to say, "Whether you are a doctor, lawyer, business man or a teacher, where your knowledge ends, God's knowledge begins. Rather than question the moving of God with your limited understanding, just accept it by faith. When you move in the faith zone, the Lord will pour out His Spirit upon you and you will experience His promises and miracles in your midst." As I glanced at the congregation, the Lord pointed out to me the four men that were against the moving of the Holy Spirit. Of course, I did not point them out. That was not the reason why God revealed them to me. I believe He did this because of what was to happen in the evening service.

The song leader said, "God is doing a work here this morning. Let us continue to praise Him." I quietly went back to my seat. There was a visiting couple sitting in the front row. Within minutes, the wife came up to the front of the church. The pastor turned to her and said, "Is there something you want to say?" She first told the pastor that they were Mr. and Mrs. Jones. The congregation, knowing that they were famous artists in that area, all looked at each other in amazement. The woman continued to tell the pastor, "I just want you to know that my husband and I have been saved for three years. This morning as we were praying before breakfast, asking God how we can serve Him. The Lord spoke to us and said, if we came to your church, we would get our answer. My husband and I are both artists. I want you to know that we did get our answer this morning through that woman who just gave the art illustration. God through her has shown us how we can serve Him using our field of art."

I was sure by this time that the congregation was baffled by the way God was working in the service. It was the first time God had used this woman to bring forth the message in tongues. I heard later that day, that she was a close friend of the four men that God had shown me that morning. That should have been enough to convince the men that the Holy Spirit was working. Secondly, the Lord used me, an outsider, to bring forth a Word of Knowledge. Lastly, two famous artists, attending the service for the first time, received from God the answer to their prayer through the workings of the Holy Spirit.

What more did God have to do to convince the congregation? God revealed in various ways the importance of the gifts of the Holy Spirit operating in the church. He wanted to let them know how much He loved them and wanted them to be free in the Spirit.

The pastor turned the service over to my husband to preach the sermon. At the end of the sermon, many people went up for prayer. God's healing power was manifested as we prayed.

There was one miracle that stands out in my mind. The youth pastor came up with his two-year-old daughter for prayer. The child had a sickness that caused her hair to fall out. They couldn't even comb her hair without losing some of her hair. We prayed and God healed her! In the evening service the pastor gave this wonderful healing testimony. He said, "We combed our daughter's hair this afternoon and not one hair fell out from her head. Praise God!"

This wasn't the half of what God did that day. We were invited to the pastor's home for dinner. That was when I was first introduced to him. He shared with us that for two years the moving of the Holy Spirit was quenched and inhibited. He said, "There was a breakthrough this morning. We have been praying for this for a long time." He then shared with us that they had asked him to resign as pastor a few weeks earlier.

It all became clear to me why God worked and moved in the morning service the way He did.

That night, before the evening service began, I entered into the lobby of the church. Two deacons approached me and asked me if I would like a cup of coffee. I instantly recognized them as two of the four men that God had shown me in the morning service. They were

238

being overly polite and friendly. I thought, "Oh Lord, what is this all about?" By now they knew who I was.

One of the men said, "Sister Franco, did you know anything about our church before the service?"

"No, brother, I didn't know anything about your church, and hadn't even met your pastor until after the service. I set up the tapes and came into the service without talking to anyone."

"My, that was something that took place this morning!"

I told him, "The Lord must really love you people. It is rare that God moves so mightily in a service like He did this morning. You should feel privileged and thankful for this wonderful visitation from the Holy Spirit."

The evening service started. A revival had begun! My husband was unable to preach. He told them, "God wants to move in a special way, and we should not stand in the way. We will allow the Holy Spirit to have full preeminence in our midst." People were testifying about the different healings that had occurred in the morning service.

At the end of the evening service, all the young people and some adults came up to the altar for prayer. Thirteen people received the infilling of the Holy Spirit. You can never guess who came up to help pray for the people. Yes, the four men who were against the moving of the Holy Spirit! They were at the altar praying for others and being filled with the Holy Spirit.

Revival will come when we go beyond our limited understanding, enter into the realm of faith and allow the Holy Spirit to move.

Truth Revealed Through Prophecy

Prophecy is one of the gifts of the Holy Spirit. In my own experience God gave me a Word of Prophecy that delivered a family from destruction.

We were asked to pray about this situation. It was a case of false accusation that seemed like a hopeless case. But God had given me a Word of Knowledge through the inspiration of the Holy Spirit confirming that He would defend and deliver this family. Finally, the night before there was to be a trial, we prayed to God through Jesus Christ and in the power of the Holy Spirit knowing that the only solution for a miracle of deliverance had to come from God and Him alone. As we read some of the Psalms in faith believing, we asked God to intervene on behalf of this family, even as He delivered and defended David of old.

After praying, we went to bed early that night. The next morning we were to accompany the family to the courthouse. At three o'clock that morning I was awakened with a prophecy from the Lord. I said to the Lord, "I just can't remember it all."

Then a voice in my spirit said, *"Arise and write it down on paper and give it to all those who stand in judgment."* I followed the leading of the Holy Spirit and wrote the words down on paper.

I prefaced the prophecy with the following opening paragraph. I wrote, "To those who stand in Judgment, let it be known that early this morning I was awakened from my sleep with a prophecy from God, as you will find in the court Bible in I Corinthians 12:10 and in I Corinthians 14:3. In obedience to the Word of God I must pass it unto you in Love." Then on the back of the paper I wrote out the Bible verses. "To another the working of miracles; to another prophecy; to another discerning of spirits; to another the interpretation of tongues:" "But he that prohesieth speaketh unto men to edification, and exhortation, and comfort."

This is a copy of the prophecy as it was given by God, *"Ye men and women of the law who sitteth in high places, I speak to thee in a voice of thunder, for thou useth my word (the Bible) in thy courts as a symbol of truth and yet thou seeketh not to know the truth. But thou believeth what thou heareth and thou maketh judgement upon my children. Yea, I say unto thee, I am the Lord God, who sitteth in the highest judgment seat, who knows the heart of man and judgeth in the light of the truth, not in the appearance thereof. Counselors of the law, I say unto thee go slowly, not in haste and the truth will be revealed unto thee. Pass not judgment swiftly for the acclaim of men and for the swelling up of oneself, for thou cometh strongly, saying thou knoweth the truth, but thou knoweth not the truth and thou putteth much spoil to what I have made good. I bring deliverance, not condemnation. Make not little of what I say unto thee, for thou who maketh judgment will be judged in that day. Therefore think much upon my counsel I say unto thee."*

I told the Lord I would obey His leading. I had three copies of the prophecy with me. I did not share this with anyone for fear that they wouldn't understand. But when we dare to obey God, He will do the impossible and bring about a miracle that only He is capable of doing.

We were in the waiting room when the attorney arrived. I asked God to let me know when I should give the written prophecy to him. I felt strongly, "Not yet, wait!" The attorney approached the defendant and offered a fabricated untruth about the incident. That moment I was reminded of what the Lord gave me through the word the night before, *"He will look into their eyes and not be afraid, for he will not speak. I will speak through him."*

Immediately the defendant rejected the offer and said, "I will not lie for you or anyone." When the attorney heard this, he became very nervous. He walked away from the defendant and stood alone by a window puffing on a cigarette. I believe that God was already convicting him of distorting the truth at the cost of destroying an innocent person.

Then the Lord said to me, *"Go. Now is the time."* I approached the attorney and told him that God gave me this message to give to him, the other attorney and to the judge. He freely took the paper from me and began reading it while I waited there. As he finished reading the prophecy and the Biblical scriptures written on the back of the page, with watery eyes, he looked at me and said, "May I keep this? I will always carry it in my briefcase." He went on to tell me, "I am removing myself from this case. I owed the prosecuting attorney a favor and if she won this case, she would be promoted to a state position. But after reading this paper, I can't go through with her plan." He went over to the defendant, and said, "As of now I am off your case because I know you are innocent and you will be cleared."

God revealed the truth through prophecy and turned the whole situation around. God works in mysterious ways, His wonders to perform!

That court hearing was canceled and God brought about a miracle of deliverance. We were with the defendant when they met this attorney a week later, and with an excitable voice he looked toward me and grabbed my hand.

Then he said, "Mrs. Franco, I must tell you what happened. Last week my wife's car was totaled and no one can understand how both my wife and children were not killed in that accident. They came out of the accident without any injuries."

I told him, "I believe God gave you a miracle and spared your family because you obeyed Him rather than man by taking a stand for the truth. You have much to be thankful for."

"Yes, I will never forget this."

Through prayer, God brought forth His word revealing the truth. The message was delivered, received and put into action bringing about two miracles of deliverance. Satan was out to destroy these families, but God proved once again through divine intervention that there is no power greater than God!

What brought about this wonderful miracle? A miracle of this nature could have only come about by the unwavering faith of the Christians who had prayed with unrelenting belief despite the odds.

By faith they unlocked the door to the supernatural, unleashing the Holy Spirit and the gifts to operate, making this miracle a possibility. When all hope seems to be gone, hold fast to the God of the impossible. Only He can make a way where there seems to be no way.

One Last Word....

Now that you have walked along with me through my lifetime of experiencing miracles, I trust that you have seen how the Holy Spirit works through the body, mind and spirit to bring about a miracle.

If you are in need of a miracle, whether it be for healing, salvation, deliverance or provision, pray in faith believing that all things are possible with God, and what he has done for me and countless others, He can do for you!

The greatest miracle of all is the salvation of the soul that prepares us for heaven. When you started reading this book, if you did not know Christ as your personal Savior, I trust that He has been revealed to you through these pages. This may be your last opportunity to receive Him as your Lord and Savior. Just repeat this simple prayer and find a good Bible teaching church to attend:

Jesus, I believe in my heart that you are the Son of God,
and that you died on the cross for all my sins.
I repent and I ask forgiveness for all of my sins and
I want to be born again. I invite you into my heart and life as
Lord and Savior. Thank you God for my miracle of salvation,
the gift of eternal life, in Jesus Name, Amen!